Financial Accounting

Concepts and Applications

VOLUME II: TEXT

Financial Accounting

Concepts and Applications

VOLUME II: TEXT

DR. V K GOYAL
M.Com., LL.B., Ph.D.(Delhi)
Reader in Commerce
Shri Ram College of Commerce
Delhi

EXCEL BOOKS

ISBN 81-7446-493-X

First Edition: New Delhi, 2006

EXCEL BOOKS
A-45, Naraina, Phase I,
New Delhi - 110 028

Published by Anurag Jain for Excel Books, A-45, Naraina, Phase I, New Delhi-110 028
and printed by him at Excel Printers, C-206, Naraina, Phase I, New Delhi - 110 028

Dedicated to

The Almighty
and
My Parents

Contents

Preface

It is indeed a privilege to write a book on Accounting. This book has been written as per latest and revised syllabus for B.Com. course of Delhi University and other Indian universities.

This book is prepared for the students and teachers to serve as a text and a source to provide a detailed and varied coverage of different topics in a simple and sequential format.

The special feature of the book is its simple and systematic approach.

The other salient features of the book are—

1. The language is very simple and lucid
2. Sufficient number of problems are given in a graded manner as solved illustrations.
3. Latest Delhi University and other professional institutes' examination questions up to 2006 are taken care of.
4. The subject matter is divided into two volumes, i.e., Volume 1 for text and Volume II for assignments along with answers for the sake of students' convenience i.e. easy to carry each volume as per one's requirement.
5. All types of questions such as essay type questions, objective type questions, are added in abundance along with large number of unsolved questions in the form of exercises.

My sincere gratitude and thanks to all my dear friends and colleagues of SRCC and those in other colleges.

I would also like to thank Mr. Anurag Jain, the publisher, of his involvement, without whose active support it would not be possible to publish this book on time and in such a beautiful manner.

I hope the readers would find it helpful and useful.

Constructive suggestions for further improvement of the book are welcome.

Dr. V K Goyal

CHAPTER 1

MEANING AND OBJECTIVES OF ACCOUNTING AND ACCOUNTING INFORMATION

A. Essay Type Questions

1. Define Accounting. What are its objectives and limitations?
2. What is accounting? Explain its main characteristics.
3. Distinguish between
   (i) Book keeping and accounting [Delhi, B. Com. (Pass) 2006 (B)]
   (ii) Accrual basis and cash basis of accounting [Delhi, B. Com. (Pass) 1999,(B), 2003]
4. Accounting is indispensable. Do you agree with this statement? Explain the role of accounting.
5. Explain the concept of accounting information.
6. How accounting is related with economics? Explain.
7. Enumerate the various users of accounting information.
8. State the meaning and objective of accounting. [Delhi, B. Com. (pass) 1991]
9. Define accounting. In what way is accounting information useful for (i) owners (ii) managers (iii) creditors and (iv) employees of a business?
10. Utility of Accounting Information. [Delhi, B. Com (Pass), 1999]

B. Objective Type Questions

I. State whether the following statements are true or false.
   (a) Accounting is the language of business.
   (b) An increase in assets is not due to profits.
   (c) Accounting deals with the information which can be measured in money or money's worth.
   (d) The term book keeping and accountancy can be used interchangeably.
   (e) Accounting deals in recording only of business transactions.
   (f) Profit increase capital.
   (g) Accounting is a service function.
   (h) Accounting deals with those events and transactions which are of financial nature.
   (i) Drawing increase capital.
   (j) Capital means total Assets-total liabilities.

II. Fill in the blanks.
   (a) In accounting transactions and events which are of ____________ are recorded.
   (b) The objective of accounting information is to provide ______________ view of the business
   (c) Where ____ ends _______ begins.
   (d) The person to whom goods are sold on credit is known as ___________
   (e) The person from whom goods are purchased on credit are known as _______
   (f) Goods/money taken for personal use is termed as ________
   (g) Accounting is a substitute of ___________
   (h) The objective of financial accounting is to ascertain ______ for a particular period.
   (i) The balance sheet is _______ statement.

III Indicate the correct answer in the following cases :

(a) A person who brings capital in the business is called ______

(1) A debtor

(2) A creditor

(3) Proprietor

(4) None of the above

(b) A person who supplies goods to the firm is known as ___

(1) A debtor

(2) A creditor

(3) The owner

(4) None of the above

(c) A person who owes money to the firm is known as ___

(1) Adebtor

(2) A creditor

(3) None of the above.

(d) Investment is taken as

(1) Current assets

(2) Fixed assets

(3) None of the above.

ANSWERS

B. Objective type Questions

I. True or False

True (a), (b), (c), (d), (f), (g), (h), (j)

False (e) (i)

III. Fill in the blanks

(i) Financial Nature

(ii) True and Fair

(iii) Book keeping, Accounting

(iv) The debtor

(v) The creditor

(vi) Drawings

(vii) Memory

(viii) Profit/loss

(ix) Position

IV. Indicate the correct answer

(a) III

(b) II

(c) I

(d) I if shown with current assets.

CHAPTER 2

THEORY BASE OF ACCOUNTING AND ACCOUNTING STANDARDS

A. Essay Type Questions-

1. What do you understand by generally accepted accounting principles? Briefly state the various concepts and convention of Accounting.
2. What are the accounting concepts and conventions? Name them and explain any two accounting concepts in detail.
3. Specify basic concepts and conventions! Is there any clash between consistency and conservatism? Elucidate.
4. Explain Various accounting principles. Discuss their significance and limitations.
5. Explain briefly the concept of materiality. Give examples. [Delhi B.Com (Pass) 1993, 2004]
6. Explain:
   (a) Business Entity concept
   [Delhi B.Com (Pass) 1997, 2002B]
   (b) Money Measurement concept
   [Delhi B.Com (Pass) 2002B, 2005 & 2006]
   (c) Accounting Period Concept.
   [Delhi B.Com (Pass) 1998]
   (d) Going Concern Concept.
   [Delhi B.Com (Pass) 1999(B), 2003, 2004, 2005 & 2006]
   (e) Dual Aspect Concept
   [Delhi B.Com (Pass) 2000 & 2002]
   (f) Matching Concept [Matching of Cost and Revenues]
   [Delhi B.Com (Pass) 2003]
   (g) Convention of Conservatism
   [Delhi B.Com (Pass) 1999,2001(B), 2002, 2005 & 2006]
   (h) Convention of consistency
   [Delhi B.Com (Pass) 1998, 2000(B), 2001 & 2006]
   (i) Convention of full disclosure
   [Delhi, B.Com (Pass), 1997 & 2006]
   (j) Accrual and cash basis
   [Delhi, B.Com (Pass), 2003]
7. "Accounting is the language of business." Explain it and discuss any four concepts of Accounting.
   [C.S.S. Meerut, BBA II Sem,.1997]
8. What do you understand by Accounting standards? Explain and also discuss in brief the need for such standards.
9. How many Accounting Standards are given by the Institute of Chartered Accountants of India? And how many of them are made mandatory. Explain.

B. Objective Type Questions

1. State whether the following statements are true or false:
   (a) All the transactions are recorded in Accounting whether expressed in terms of money or not?
   (b) Recording of each transactions is done at two places according to dual aspect concept.
   (c) Revenue is matched with expenses.
   (d) All the changes are taken into account as per money measurement concept/assumption.
2. Fill in the blanks :
   (a) Generally accepted accounting principles is a set of .... accepted rules. (Commonly, uncommon)
   (b) Business is a .... entity. (Separate, mixed)
   (c) Only such transactions are recorded which .... in money. (are not measured, are measured)
   (d) Going concern states that business has a .... life. (Definite, Indefinite)
   (e) AS-2- Valuation of Inventions is .... Accounting Standard (Mandatory, Not Mandatory)
   (f) AS-3- Cash Flow Statement is .... Accounting Standard (Mandatory, Not Mandatory)
3. Assign reasons:
   (i) To present accounts in such a way which can give us true and fair view of the business.
   (ii) Yes, it is necessary to record drawings with a view to ascertain true profit or loss
   (iii) The life of business is assumed to be indefinite (going concern concept) yet companies prepare their accounts annually. What is the basis?
   [Delhi B.Com (Pass), 2006(B)]
   (iv) The proprietor has withdrawn some goods from the business for his personal use. It is compulsory to record it in the books of the firm? Give reasons?
   [Delhi B.Com (Pass), 2006(B)]

ANSWERS

Objective Type Questions -

(1) (a) False (b) True (c) True (d) False

(2) (a) Commonly (b) separate (c) are measured (d) Indefinite
(e) Mandatory (f) Not Mandatory.

CHAPTER 3

SOURCE DOCUMENTS AND ACCOUNTING EQUATION

A. Essay Type Questions

1. What do you understand by source documents? What purpose do they serve? Give three examples of source documents.
2. Define accounting equation. Explain the basis or important concept on which it is formed.
3. 'Accounting equation holds true under all the circumstances. Do you agree with this statement? Give few examples to justify your statement.
4. What is owner's equity?
5. Explain in short, the meaning of 'Accounting Equation.'

   [Delhi B Com. (Pass) 2005]
6. Describe the fundamental accounting equation. How are revenue and expense accounts related to it?
7. Explain the method for computation of accounting equation.

B. Objective Type Questions

1. Explain which is true or false?
   (a) Assets = Capital + Liabilities
   (b) Capital = Assets - Liabilities
   (c) Liabilities = Assets - Capital
2. Fill in the blanks :
   (a) If the total Assets of a business are Rs. 50,000 capital contributed by A is Rs. .... If loan capital is Rs. 35,000.
      (i) Rs. 10,000 (ii) Rs. 15,000 (iii) Rs. 35,000
   (b) If capital contributed is Rs. 75,000 and loan capital is Rs. 17,500, the assets of the business are Rs.............
      (i) Rs. 57,500 (ii) Rs. 92,500 (iii) Rs. 60,000
   (c) Find out the amount of loan capital from the following :
      (i) Assets are worth Rs. 1,50,000
      (ii) Capital contributed by the owner Rs. 52,500
      (iii) Loan capital is Rs. .....
      (i) Rs. 2,02,500 (ii) Rs. 52,500 (iii) Rs. 97,500
3. Point out whether the following statements are true or false.
   (i) Owner's equity represents the capital brought in by the Owner + Accumulated profits.
   (ii) Owner's equity represents the capital brought in by the Owner + Outsiders.
   (iii) Owner's equity represents the loan capital only.
4. Find out the amount of total assets from the following details :
   (i) Capital brought in Rs 1,00,000
   (ii) Loan capital Rs. 25,000
   (iii) Profit earned during the period Rs. 17,500
   (iv) Depreciation to be charged during the period Rs. 2,000.

   Total Assets are Rs. ....

   (a) Rs. 1,25,000 (b) Rs. 1,42,500 (c) Rs. 1,40,500

5. Fill in the blanks.

Assets = Capital + Liabilities

	Rs.		Rs.		Rs.
(i)	1,25,000	=	75,000	+	?
(ii)	2,00,000	=	?	+	1,45,000
(iii)	?	=	50,000	+	77,500

6. Point out the effect on Accounting equation whether there is an increase or decrease or no effect.
   (i) Purchase of goods for cash.
   (ii) Purchase of goods on credit
   (iii) Sale of goods on credit
   (iv) Purchase of furniture on credit
   (v) Sale of old plant for cash
   (vi) Rent paid
   (vii) Dividend received in cash
   (viii) Income tax paid

C. Exercises

1. Develop accounting equation from the following transactions:

		R s.
(i)	Mohan commenced business with cash	50,000
(ii)	Purchased goods for cash	30,000
(iii)	Purchased goods on credit	20,000
(iv)	Sold goods (cost Rs. 10,000) for	12,000
(v)	Bought furniture on credit	2,000
(vi)	Paid cash to a creditor	15,000

2. Show the accounting equation on the basis of the following transactions:

		Rs.
(i)	Ram started business with	25,000
(ii)	Purchased goods from Shyam	10,000
(iii)	Sold goods to Sohan costing Rs. 1,500 for	1,800

3. Show the accounting equation on the basis of the following transactions:

		Rs.
(i)	P & Co. started business with	20,000
(ii)	Purchased goods on credit with	5,000
(iii)	Sold goods to G. Rai on credit costing Rs. 1,000 for	1,200

4. Develop accounting equation from the following transaction:

		Rs.
(i)	Rakesh started business with	1,00,000
(ii)	Purchased furniture for cash	12,500
(iii)	Purchased Goods on credit from Mukesh worth	27,250
(iv)	Sold Goods to Roop on credit if costing Rs. 20,000	25,000
(v)	Paid Rent	1,500
(vi)	Depreciation to be charged on furniture	1,250
(vii)	Withdrew cash for personal use	6,000

ANSWERS

Objective Type Questions

1. (a) True
   (b) False
   (c) False
2. (a) (ii) Rs. 15,000
   (b) (ii) Rs. 92,500
   (c) (iii) Rs. 97,500
3. (1) True
   (2) False
   (3) False
4. Amount of total Assets (c) Rs. 1,40,500
5. (i) Rs. 50,000
   (ii) Rs. 55,000
   (iii) Rs. 1,27,500
6. (i) No effect
   (ii) Increase in Assets as well as Liabilities
   (iii) No effect
   (iv) Increase in Assets as well as liabilities
   (v) No effect
   (vi) Decrease in Assets as well as capital
   (vii) Increase in Assets as well as liabilities
   (viii) Decrease in Assets as well as capital

Exercises

1.	Assets	Rs.	59,000	= Cap. Rs. 52,000 + Lia	Rs.	7,000
2.	Assets	Rs.	35,300	= Cap. Rs. 25,300 + Lia.	Rs.	10,000
3.	Assets	Rs.	25,200	= Cap. Rs. 20,200 + Lia	Rs.	5,000
4.	Assets	Rs.	1,23,500	= Cap. Rs. 96,250 + Lia	Rs.	27,250

CHAPTER 4

ACCOUNTING PROCESS

A. Essay type Questions

1. What is an account? What purpose does it serve to the business? Explain with suitable example.
2. Distinguish between personal and Impersonal Accounts.
3. How are accounts classified? Give two examples in each case.
4. What do you understand by the following Statement that every debit has a credit'. Explain fully with suitable examples.
5. Explain the rules of debit and credit in case of nominal accounts, giving suitable examples.
6. What is double entry system of Book keeping? Discuss fully this concept.
7. State the principles of Double Entry system of Accounting. Give briefly its chief advantages.
8. Write the merits and demerits of Double Entry system of Accounting. Explain.
9. 'Every debit must have a corresponding credit' Explain.

B. Objective Type Questions

1. Fill in the Blanks

(a) Capital is a	(i) Personal	(ii) Real	(iii) Nominal A/c
(b) Drawings is a	(i) Personal	(ii) Real	(iii) Nominal A/c
(c) Furniture is a	(i) Personal	(ii) Real	(iii) Nominal A/c
(d) State Bank of India is a	(i) Personal	(ii) Real	(iii) Nominal A/c
(e) Rent paid is a.......	(i) Personal	(ii) Real	(iii) Nominal A/c

2. (I) Which A/c is to be debited:

(i) If furniture is purchased for cash	(i) Furniture A/c (ii) Cash A/c
(ii) If goods are sold for cash.	(i) Goods A/c (ii) Cash A/c
(iii) If expenses are paid in cash	(i) Expenses A/c (ii) Cash A/c
(iv) If commission is accrued but not received	(i) Income (commission) (ii) Commission Accrued

(II) Which A/c is to be credited:

(i) Rs. 10,000 paid to Bank	(i) cash A/c	(ii) Bank A/c
(ii) Withdrew for personal A/c	(i) Drawings A/c	(ii) cash/Bank A/c
(iii) Rent is outstanding but not paid	(i) Rent A/c	(ii) Rent outstanding
(iv) Goods purchased on credit from Ram	(i) Goods A/c	(ii) Ram

(I) State whether the following statement is true or false.

(i) Rent paid is personal A/c

(ii) Bad debt is a loss to the business.

(iii) Capital is an income to the business.

(iv) Furniture is a Real Account.

(v) Compound entry can be passed when number of accounts involved is more than two.

(vi) Double Entry System of accounting is suitable to all the business concerns.

(vii) The journal is the main books of the business.

C. Exercises

1. Classify the following accounts under three types of accounts-

(i) Rent A/c	(ii) Ashish Kumar	(iii) B.H.U.
(iv) Wages A/c	(v) Dividend Received	(vi) interest owing A/c
(vii) Furniture A/c	(viii) Depreciation A/c	(ix) Loan
(x) Sales A/c		

2. From the following transactions, find out the two relevant accounts & classify them under three types of accounts:
   (i) Furniture purchased for Rs. 10,000 from M/s Delite Furniture House, Delhi.
   (ii) Paid cartage Rs. 500 for furniture.
   (iii) Paid Rs. 7,500 to M/s Delite Furniture House, Delhi.
   (iv) Paid Rs. 1,500 as interest to the seller of goods.
3. From the following Transactions, prepare an account of the proprietor:

	Rs.
(i) Business started with cash	50,000
(ii) Drawings during the year @ Rs. 1000 per month	
(iii) Introduced additional capital	17,000
(iv) Net profit as per profit and loss a/c	5,500

4. From the following Transactions, prepare a furniture account:

	Rs.
(i) Furniture purchased	25,000
(ii) Furniture purchased	12,000
(iii) Furniture sold	5,000
(iv) Depreciation on Furniture	2,000

5. Classify the following transactions into different categories of accounts as per Modern Classification:

	Rs.
(i) Business Started with cash	1,00,000
(ii) Furniture purchased	12,000
(iii) Goods Purchased from Ashish	50,000
(iv) Goods sold to Nishank	25,000
(v) Rent paid	5,000
(vi) Interest Received	1,000
(vii) Withdrew for personal use	15,000

ANSWERS

B. Objective Type Questions

1. (a) I (b) I (c) II (d) I (e) III

2. 1. (I) (i), (II) (ii)
(III) (i), (IV) (ii)

II. (I) I (II) II (III) II (IV) II

III (1) False (2) True (3) False (4) True
(5) True (6) False (7) True

C. Exercises

1. (i) N (ii) P (iii) P (iv) N
   (v) N (vi) P (vii) R (viii) N
   (ix) P (x) R

2. (I)	(a) Furniture A/c	....	R
	(b) Delite Furniture A/c	....	P
(II)	(a) Cartage A/c	....	N
	(b) Cash A/c	....	R
(III)	(a) Delite Furniture A/c	....	P
	(b) Cash A/c	....	R
(IV)	(a) Interest A/c	....	N
	(b) Cash A/c	....	R

3) Closing Balance Rs. 60,500

4) Balance of Furniture a/c Rs. 30,000

5) (i) Asset, Capital
   (ii) Asset
   (iii) Asset
   (iv) Asset
   (v) Expenses
   (vi) Revenue (Income)
   (vii) Capital

CHAPTER 5

SOURCE DOCUMENTS AND VOUCHERS FOR RECORDING OF TRANSACTIONS

A. Essay type Questions-

1. What is journal? Which transactions are usually recorded in it? Give three examples of such transactions.
2. What do you understand by the following statement that every debit has a credit? Explain fully with suitable examples.
3. Name the three types of accounts. Give their respective rules of journalising the transactions.
4. Is the journal a book of original entry? Explain briefly
5. Define Journal explain its advantages and limitations.
6. Define a ledger. Explain its importance.
7. Distinguish between a journal and a ledger.
8. What is a ledger? Why it is called chief book of accounts?
9. What is posting? Explain the rules of posting from journal to ledger accounts.
10. What is meant by balancing of an account?
11. What is an account? Give important types of accounts along with rules of journalisation.

B. Objective Type of Questions

1. Fill in the blanks

(a) Capital is a........	(i) Personal	(ii) Real	(iii)Nominal A/c
(b) Drawings is a.......	(i) Personal	(ii) Real	(iii)Nominal A/c
(c) Furniture is a......	(i) Personal	(ii) Real	(iii) Nominal a/c
(d) State Bank of India is....	(i) Personal	(ii) Real	(iii) Nominal a/c
(e) Rent paid is a.....	(i) Personal	(ii) Real	(iii) Nominal a/c

2. (1) Which A/c is to be debited:

(i) If Furniture is purchased for cash.
   (i) Furniture A/c (ii) Cash A/c

(ii) If goods are sold for cash
   (i) Goods A/c (ii) Cash A/c

(iii) If Expenses are paid in cash
   (i) Expenses A/c (ii) Cash A/c

(iv) If commission is accrued but not received.
   (i) Income (commission) (ii) Commission Accrued

(II) Which A/c is to be credited?

(i) Rs. 10,000 paid to Bank
(i) Cash A/c (ii) Bank A/c
(ii) Withdrew for personal A/c
(i) Drawings A/c (ii) Cash/Bank A/c
(iii) Rent is outstanding but not paid.
(i) Rent A/c (ii) Rent outstanding

(iv) Goods purchased on credit from Ram.

(i) Goods A/c (ii) Ram

C. Exercises

1. Journalise the following in the books of Ram

Date	Particulars	Rs.
2006		
July 12	Bought goods from Rakesh	10,000
July 15	Trade expenses paid	1,200
July 18	Wages paid	120
July 20	Paid Rakesh in full settlement of his account	9,750
July 27	Received cash from Mukesh	11,500
	allowed him discount	500
July 28	Paid interest on Capital	1,500
July 31	Rent paid	750

2. Kishore's books disclosed the following opening balance of 1st January 2006

Assets	Rs.	Liabilities	Rs.
Cash in hand	400	Sundry Creditors	
Cash at Bank	4,500	Ram	1500
Stock	4,500	Shayam	2800
Furniture	1,500	Ghanshyam	340
Sundry Debtors		Hari	170
Krishan	2,000		
sanjay	510		

During the month ending January 2006 the following transactions took place:

Date	Particulars	Rs.
2006		
Jan 1	Sold goods for cash	1,500
Jan 4	Purchased goods from Sanjay	2,000
Jan 5	Paid to Sanjay	1,500
Jan 6	Deposited in Bank	250
Jan 7	Paid for Postage	50
Jan 8	Krishan paid by cheque in full settlement of his A/c	1,950
Jan 15	Sold goods on credit to Ram	1,200
Jan 18	Withdrew from Bank	2,000
Jan 20	Cash sales	4,750
Jan 25	Cash purchases	2,575
Jan 27	Paid salaries	1,200
Jan 31	Paid rent	500

You are required to journalise the above transactions.

3. Journalise the following transactions in the books of Mr. Rakesh Kumar.

Date	Particulars	Rs.
2006		
July 1	Started business with a capital of	20,000
July 2	Purchased a typewriter for	450
July 3	Bought goods on credit from Sanjay	10,000
July 4	Purchased Postage Stamps	50
July 5	Sold goods for cash	750
July 7	Sold Goods to Mukesh on credit	1,250
July 8	Paid to Sanjay	8,500
July 9	Goods returned to Sanjay	500
July 12	Paid into Bank	10,000
July 15	Received from Mukesh in full settlement of his A/c	1,175
July 19	Electricity paid	525
July 23	Office stationary purchased for	1,000
July 25	Goods purchased for cash payment was by cheque	5,000
July 28	Cash Sales	2,200
July 29	Rent Paid	1,000
July 29	Salary paid	2,500
July 30	Insurance Premium paid	750
July 31	Withdraw from Bank for personal use	2,500

4. Roop's books disclosed the following opening balances as on 1st January 2006

Assets	Rs.
Furniture	5,000
Stock	8,000
Machinery	10,000
Cash in hand	3,000
Cash at Bank	12,500
Amount due from Debtors	15,000
Liability	
Amount due to Goyal Distributors	25,000
Amount due to Sharma Stores	1,500
Amount due to Krishna Ltd.	3,500

During the month, ending January 2006 the following transactions took place:

Date	Particulars	Rs.
2006		
Jan 1	Goods sold for cash	10,000
Jan 4	Purchased goods on credit from Ram Lal	5,000
Jan 7	Paid to Ram Lal by cheque	5,000
Jan 10	Cartage paid	250
Jan 12	Deposited in a Bank	3,000
Jan 14	Goods sold to Bantoo	15,000
Jan 16	Received cash from Bantoo	12,000
Jan 17	Cash sales	5,500
Jan 18	Paid cartage	275
Jan 20	Paid Telephone bills	380
Jan 21	Received a cheque from Bantoo	2,900
Jan 22	Goods sold to Raju	1,500
Jan 24	Received a cheque from Raju	1,500
Jan 25	Purchased goods on credit from C. Lal & Sons	2,900
Jan 26	Issued a cheque to C. Lal & Sons for	2,850
Jan 29	Goods sold for cash	5,000
Jan 31	Paid salaries	2,500
Jan 31	Purchased Govt. Bonds	5,000
Jan 31	Insurance Premium paid by cheque	1,000

Pass necessary journal entries with narration.

05. Prepare Rama Rao's Account on 31st March 2006 by taking relevant transactions in the books of Mr Naidu.

Date	Particulars	Rs.
2006		
March 1	Amount due to Rama Rao	5,000
March 5	Cash sales to Rama Rao	1,500
March 7	Credit sales to Rama rao	4,000
March 10	Returned goods to khan	500
March 15	Goods returned by Rama Rao	1,000
March 31	Mr. Naidu settled the balance due to Rama Rao by a bank draft	

06. Write up Sundram's account from the following particulars

Date	Particulars	Rs.
2006		
March 1	Amount due from Sundram	4,000
March 4	Cash sales to Sundram	1,400
March 10	Goods Returned to Mr, Malik	200
March 15	Sundram purchased goods from us	2400
March 18	Goods returned by Sundram	300
March 22	Cash purchases.	1500
March 31	Sundram settled discount and was allowed discount	30

ANSWERS

B. Objective type Questions-

1. (a) (1) (b) I (c) II (d) I (e) III
2. (i) (i) (i) (ii) (i) (i)

   (ii) (ii) (ii) (ii)

   (iii) (I) (iii) (ii)

   (iv) (ii) (iv) (ii)

C. Exercises

5. Balance of Mr. Rama Rao's a/c Rs. 2,000.
6. Balance of Mr. Sundaram's a/c Rs. 1,870.

CHAPTER 6

SUBSIDIARY BOOKS OF BUSINESS

A. Essay Type Questions

1. Briefly explain the important books of the business.
2. What do you understand by subsidiary books? Describe the object of preparing them.
   [Delhi B.Com (Pass) 1999, 2001
3. What do you understand by special purpose subsidiary books? Give the ruling of one such book.
   [Delhi B. Com (Pass) 2001-2004]
4. Why is the journal sub-divided in a large business house? List four specialized (subsidiary) journal and give the functions of each.
5. What is Cash Book? Discuss its types and uses.
6. Cash book is a journal and a ledger. Explain.
   [Delhi B.Com (Pass) 2003]
7. What is cash discount? Distinguish it from trade discount.
   [Delhi B.Com (Pass) 2001 (B) 2002(B) 2004 & 2005, 2006 (B)]
8. What is 'Contra entry'? How will you recognize it from among other entries in Cash Book?
   [Delhi, B.Com. (Pass) 2006 (B)]
9. Explain the meaning of Imprest system of Cash Book.
   [Delhi B.Com (Pass) 2000(B) & 2001 (B)
10. What is meant by posting? How would you post?
    (i) Purchases Book
    (ii) Sales Book.
11. Name the various entries which have to be passed through a journal even though we might have kept all the subsidiary books.

B. Objective Type Questions

1. State which of the following statements are True of False :
   (i) Cash sales are recorded in Sales Day Book.
   (ii) Credit sales are recorded in Sales Day Book.
   (iii) Cash and credit sales are recorded in Sales Day Book.
   (iv) Purchase of fixed asset is recorded in the Purchases Day Book.
   (v) Credit purchase of raw material is recorded in the Purchases day Book.
   (vi) Petty Cash Book is handled by the Head Cashier.
   (vii) Petty Cash Book is maintained by a person known as Petty Cashier.
   (viii) The Cash Book records all cash payments only.
   (ix) The Cash Book records all cash payments and all receipts only.
2. Fill in the blanks :
   (i) The Sales Day Book records ....
      (a) all sales.
      (b) credit sales
      (c) cash sales
   (ii) The Sales Return Book records ....
      (a) the return of goods by the firm.

(b) The return of goods by the customers.

(c) The return of assets by the customers.

(iii) The total of the Purchases Day Book is posted to the ....

(a) debit of the purchases account.

(b) Credit of the sales account.

(c) Debit of the sales account.

(iv) The balance of cash account is generally ....

(a) credit

(b) debit

(c) None of these

(v) Cash discount is offered as an incentive ....

(a) for increase in volume of sales.

(b) For prompt payment.

(c) One of the above.

(vi) .... Discount is recorded in the books of the business.

(a) Cash

(b) Trade

(c) Both

(vii) Petty Cash Book is prepared generally by ....business houses.

(a) big

(b) small

(c) medium

(viii) Imprest means reimbursement of the ....

(a) full Amount advanced in the beginning.

(b) Only the amount spent.

(c) Difficult to say.

(C) Exercises

1. Prepare a Cash Book with Bank column only :

2006		Rs.
July 1	Balance at Bank	10,000
July 4	Received a cheque from Pankaj	5,000
July 7	Issued a cheque to Rakesh	6,000
July 10	Received dividend by bank draft	2,000
July 15	Mukesh was paid by issuing a cheque	1,500
July 20	Deposited into Bank	7,000
July 24	Interest collected by Bank	200
July 28	Dividend collected by Bank	500
July 31	Bank charges debited	800

2. Enter the following transactions in Cash Bank of Mr. Ashish Kumar :

2006		Rs.
July 1	Cash in hand	5,000
July 3	Received from M/s Gupta & Sons	7,000
July 5	Cash Purchases	3,500
July 7	Cash Sales	7,200
July 8	Paid Cartage	200
July 12	Paid into Bank	6,000
July 14	Cash Sales	1,250
July 20	Bought goods for Cash	2,100
July 27	Paid to Kishore	375
July 28	Paid to Naresh	550
July 29	Cash Sales	1,275
July 31	Paid Salaries	650

Double Column Cash Book

3. Enter the following Transactions into two columns Cash Book :

2006		Rs.
Aug. 1	Cash in hand	100
	Cash at Bank	890
Aug. 2	Cash Purchases	220
Aug. 3	Cash Sales	240
Aug. 4	Received from Rakesh Loan a/c	60
Aug. 5	Paid to B.D. Garg by cheque	350
Aug. 6	Additional Capital introduced	110
Aug. 6	Cash Sales	410
Aug. 6	Cash paid into Bank	480

4. From the following particulars, write out the Cash Book of M/s Goyal Traders of Muzaffar Nagar with Cash and Bank Columns and bring down the final balance on 7th June, 2006

2006		Rs.
June 1	Cash in hand	1,275.50
June 1	Cash at Bank	5,350.00
June 2	Paid Salaries	1,125.30
	Received from Maharaja & Sons	
	A cheque directly paid into Bank	650.70
June 2	Ought goods by cheque	375.00
June 4	Withdrew by cheque Cash for office	1,000.00
June 4	Paid Rakesh on account by cheque	500.00
June 6	Received in cash from Krishna Traders	1,500.00
June 6	Purchased stationery for office use	187.00
June 7	Deposited into bank from office cash	1.800.00
June 7	Cash Sales	300.00

Three column cash book

5. Compose three columns Cash Book from the following transactions :

2006		*Rs.*
Jan. 1	Cash in hand	567
Jan. 1	Cash at Bank	12,675
Jan. 2	Received from Ashish and	7,900
	Allowed him a discount	100

Contd...

2006		*Rs.*
Jan. 4	Deposited into the Bank	5,000
Jan. 6	Furniture purchased for cash	2,500
Jan. 7	Paid to Vikas by cheque	7,800
	And received discount	200
Jan. 14	Received from Manish by cheque and	
	Deposited into Bank	5,000
Jan.16	Cash Sales	8,000
Jan. 20	Deposited into bank	6,000
Jan. 25	Purchased a Machine and paid by a cheque	12,000
Jan. 26	Paid by cheque to Kishore	1,370
	and received Discount	30
Jan. 27	Withdrew from bank for office use	2,500
Jan. 28	Purchased goods for cash	5,000
Jan. 29	Paid wages by cheque	4,500
Jan. 31	Paid Rent	500

6. Enter the following transactions in the Cash Book with cash, Bank and discount columns :

1.6.06	Cash in hand	Rs. 18,000
	overdraft at Bank	Rs. 2,000
16.6.06	Rceived a cheque of Rs. 780 from P and discount allowed him Rs. 20	
17.6.06	Deposited P's cheque in the bank	
29.6.06	The cheque received from P on 16.6.06 was dishonoured.	

7. Enter the following transactions in the cash book with Cash, Bank, and discount columns :

2006		**Rs.**
Jan. 1	Cash in hand	18,000
Jan. 5	Paid into bank	7,000
Jan. 7	Received from Rakesh	700
Jan. 8	Paid wages	200
Jan. 9	Paid Mukesh by cheque	800
Jan.9	Paid for Printing	50
Jan. 10	Bought goods for cash	700
Jan. 11	Cash sales and received a cheque for it	1,000
Jan. 15	Settled Mukesh's Account for Rs. 700 by a cheque and was allowed discount Rs. 30	
Jan. 16	Received a cheque from Roop	900
Jan. 18	Received a cheque for cash sales	100
Jan. 20	Paid for on advertisement by a cheque	200
Jan. 21	Withdrew from Bank for office use	1,000
Jan. 24	Received from Anand And allowed him discount Rs. 70	2,000
Jan. 25	Drew for office use	1,000
Jan. 30	Remitted Cash to Roop on account	3,000
Jan. 30	Drew from Bank for personal use	1,000
Jan. 31	Paid for Sundry Expenses in cash	100

Petty Cash Book

8. Shri Ramaswamy maintains a columnary Petty cash book on the Imprest System. The imprest amount is Rs. 500. From, the following information, show how his petty cash book would appear for the week ended on 12th September, 2006.

2006		Rs.
Sept. 7	Balance in hand	134.90
	Received cash reimbursement to make up the imprest.	
	Postage	12.30
	Stationery	32.10
	Entertainment	5.40
Sept. 8	Travelling and Conveyance	12.60
	Miscellaneous Expenses	1.10
	Entertainment	7.20
Sept. 9	Repairs	156.70
Sept. 10	Postage	17.40
	Entertainment	12.70
	Travelling	38.40
Sept. 11	Stationery	67.30
	Entertainment	4.10
Sept. 12	Miscellaneous	1.20
	Postage	5.10
	Repairs	48.30

9. From the following particulars, write up Petty Cash Book of a trader :

2006		Rs.
Jan. 1	Petty cashier receives from the Head Cashier	100.00
Jan. 2	Paid Cartage	5.00
Jan. 3	Purchased Stationery for	25.00
Jan. 4	Purchased Carbon etc.	10.00
Jan. 5	Paid for preparing typewriter	7.50
Jan. 6	Paid for telegram	7.50
Jan. 6	Paid Telephone bill	25.00
Jan. 6	Paid Cartage	10.00

10. Rule a Petty Cash Book with four analysis columns for (1) Postage & Stationery (2) Travelling Expenses (3) Carriage and (4) Office expenses and enter up the following transactions. The Book is kept on imprest system:

The amount being Rs. 65 only.

2006		Rs.
Jan. 1	Petty Cash in hand	2.66
Jan. 1	Received Cash to make up the imprest amount	
Jan. 1	Bought stamps	5.25
Jan. 1	Paid bus fare	0.42
Jan. 2	Paid Railway fare	25.20
Jan. 2	Paid Telegram charges	4.37
Jan. 2	Bought short hand note book	0.66
Jan. 4	Paid Cartage	2.37
Jan. 5	Paid repairs to typewriter	7.37
Jan. 5	Paid Cart hire	10.25
Jan. 6	Paid office clearing	5.00

Balance the Petty Cash Book as on 6.1.06 and bring down the balance.

11. A trader starts his week on 1st April, 2006 with an opening balance of Rs. 200. His transactions during the week were as given below:

2006		Rs.
Jan. 1	Purchased Stationery	15.00
Jan. 2	Wages Paid	5.00
Jan. 2	Paid Tram fare	1.50
Jan. 2	Paid office electric bills	35.00
Jan. 3	Purchased Postage Stamps	3.50
Jan. 4	Paid for Repairs to chairs	10.50
Jan. 5	Paid Taxi fare	15.75
Jan. 6	Paid for Stationery	10.00

Enter the above in a Petty Cash Book and restore the Petty Cashier to his original balance as on 7.1.06

12. Enter the following in the Purchases Book:

2006		Rs.
Aug. 10	Bought goods from Murali Mohan	5,000
Aug. 15	Bought goods from Rama Rao	4,000
Aug. 20	Purchased goods from Gopal	8,000
Aug. 25	Purchased goods from Harikrishna for cash	10,000
Aug. 31	Purchased goods from Kavitha	6,000

13. From the following particulars write up Sales Book.

2006		Rs.
Jun. 1	Sold goods on credit to Raju	5,400
	(Trade Discount 5%)	
Jun. 10	Sold goods to Krishna on credit	7,100
	(Trade discount 8%)	
Jun. 20	Sold goods to Ganapathi	500
Jun. 25	Goods sold to Govind	8,200
	(Trade discount 4%)	

14. From the following particulars write up Sales Book.

2006		Rs.
May 1	Sold goods to Kiran on credit	5,000
	(Trade discount 10%)	
May 8	Goods sold to Murthy	12,000
	(Trade discount 5%)	
May 15	Goods sold to 'Anand' for cash	8,000
May 20	Cash sales to Kumar	5,000
	And credit sales to Kumar	10,000

15. Enter the following transactions in proper subsidiary books.

2006.		Rs.
Feb. 1	Sold Goods to Gopal Traders	3,300
Feb. 3	Sold goods to Hari & Co.	16,200
Feb. 8	Goods returned by Gopal Traders	50
Feb. 13	Sold goods to Krishna	4,200
Feb. 15	Hari & Co., returned goods	200
Feb. 18	Sold goods to Sairam	1,500
Feb. 20	Krishna returned goods	300
Feb. 28	Goods returned by Sairam	150

ANSWERS

B. Objective Type Questions

1.	(i) False	(ii) True	(iii) False	(iv) False
	(v) True	(vi) False	(vii) True	(viii) False
	(ix) True			
2.	(i) (b)	(ii) (b)	(iii) (a)	(iv) (b)
	(v) (b)	(vi) (a)	(vii) (a)	(viii) (b)

C. Exercises

Simple Single Column Cash Book

1. (i) Total of Cash Book — Rs. 24,700
   (ii) Closing Balance — Rs. 16,400
2. (i) Total of Cash Book — Rs. 21,725
   (ii) Closing Balance — Rs. 8,350

Double Columns Cash Book

3. (i) Closing Balance of Cash — Rs. 220
   (ii) Closing Balance of Bank — Rs. 1020
4. (i) Closing Balance of Cash — Rs. 963.20
   (ii) Closing Balance of Bank — Rs. 5925.70
5. (i) Closing Balance of Cash — Rs. 467
   (ii) Closing Balance of Bank — Rs. 105
6. No Change in their original balance
7. (i) Closing Balance of Cash — Rs. 11,650
   (ii) Closing Balance of Bank — Rs. 4,300

Petty Cash Book

8. Balance in hand — Rs. 78.10
9. Balance in hand — Rs. 10
10. Balance in hand — Rs. 4.11
11. Balance in hand — Rs. 103.75
12. Total of Purchases book — Rs. 23.000
13. Total of sales book — Rs. 20034
14. Total of sales book — Rs. 25900
15. (i) Total of sales book — Rs. 25200
    (ii) Total of sales Returns book — Rs. 700

CHAPTER 7

BANK RECONCILIATION STATEMENT

A. Essay type Questions

1. What is Bank Reconciliation Statement? Explain the true purpose of preparing such a statement.
2. What is a Bank Reconciliation statement? How it is prepared? Submit a Proforma example of the same.
3. Explain the reasons on account of which the balance as shown but the Bank Pass Book does not agree with the balance as shown by the bank column of the cash book.
4. How a bank reconciliation statement is prepared? What are the records necessary for preparing this statement?
5. What is Bank Reconciliation statement? Why the preparation of Bank reconciliation statement is necessary?
6. What do you mean by bank reconciliation statement? What are the reason for the difference between the balance shown by the cash book and the one show by the Pass book.

(C.S. Foundation June 1998)

B. Objective type Questions

1. State whether the following statements are true or false.
   (i) Bank reconciliation statement is prepared
      (a) to reconcile the balance of the cash book with that of the pass Book.
      (b) To reconcile the opening and closing balances of the cash book only.
      (c) To reconcile the opening and closing balances of the pass book only
      (d) None of the above.
   (ii) Cash book (bank column) is maintained by
      (a) All the business houses
      (b) All the banks.
      (c) Both the parties namely business houses and banks
2. Fill in the Blanks
   1. passbook is prepared and supplied by.........
      (i) Firm (ii) bank (iii) both
   2. Banks Reconciliation statement is prepared by...
      (i) Firm (ii) bank (iii) both
   3. The preparation of a bank Reconciliation statement is...
      (i) Compulsory (ii) optional (iii) difficult to say

C. Exercises

1. The cash book shows a balance of Rs. 12,500 on comparing the Cash Book with the Pass Book, the following discrepancies were noted-
   (i) Cheques issued but not yet presented for payment. Rs. 600
   (ii) Cheques deposited in Bank but not collected Rs. 900
   (iii) Bank paid Insurance Premium Rs. 500
   (iv) Bank charges Rs. 30
   (v) Directly deposited by a customer Rs. 800
   (vi) Interest on Investment collected by bank Rs. 200

2. On 31st December 2005, the cash Book showed a bank balance of Rs, 3,000. From the following details prepare a Bank Reconciliation Statement Showing the balance as per Pass Book.

(i) Cheques issued for Rs. 500 had not yet been presented for payment.

(ii) Cheques amounting to Rs. 700 were paid on 28th December but has not been credited by the bank. One cheque for Rs. 250 was entered in the cash book on 28th December, but banked on 3rd Jan 2006.

(iii) A cheque from Mukesh for Rs. 200 paid in on 26th December was dishonoured, but the advice was received on 3rd Jan 2006.

(iv) Bank Charges Rs. 10 debited by Bank.

(v) Bank also collected interest on deposits amounting to Rs. 400.

3. On 31st December 2005 Mr. Rakesh's Cash Book showed a bank Balance of Rs, 865 which did not agree with the balance as shown by the Pass Book. On comparison of the two, he discovers the following.

(i) He had sent cheques amounting to Rs. 13,275 of which only cheques amounting to Rs. 4050 were credited in the Pass Book.

(ii) He had given a cheque for Rs. 1260 to Mr. Roop on 15th December, which was not presented to the bank.

(iii) Rent directly deposited by the tenant Rs. 340.

(iv) Rs. 57.50 for interest was charged in the bank, which was not recorded in the cash book.

(v) A cheque for Rs. 400 which was received from a customer, was debited in the Cash Book but forgot to send it for collection to the bank.

(vi) A bill payable of Rs. 600 was duly paid off recording to Mr. Rakesh instructions, which was not recorded in the Cash Book.

4. The cash book of a merchant showed a Bank balance of Rs. 2300 as on 31st Dec 2005. On going through, the cash book, it was found that two cheques for Rs. 500 and Rs. 700 deposited in the month of December were not credited in the Pass Book till Jan 2 following and three cheques for Rs. 600 Rs. 800 and Rs 1200 issued on December 28 were not presented for payment till Jan 3 following. In addition to this, Bank had credited the merchant for Rs. 125 as interest and had debited him for Rs. 10 as bank charges for which no corresponding. Entries were made in the cash Book.

Prepare a Book Reconciliation statement as on December 31st 2005

5. From the following particulars, Prepare a bank Reconciliation statement showing the Balance as per Pass Book on 31st March 2006

(i) The Balance as per cash Book Rs. 1,80,000

(ii) Following cheques were paid in to firm a/c in March, 2006 but were credited by the bank in April 2006

A Rs. 2500, B Rs 3500 C Rs 1900

(iii) The following cheques were issued by the firm in March 2006 but were cashed in April 2006

P Rs. 2500 Q Rs. 4500 R. Rs. 4000

(iv) A cheque of Rs. 1000 which was received from a customer was entered in the bank column of the cash book in March 2006 but the same was paid into the bank in April 2006

(v) The Pass Book shows a credit Balance of Rs. 2500 for interest and a debit balance of Rs. 1000 for Bank Charges.

6. From the following particulars, Prepare a Bank reconciliation statement.

(i) Cash at Bank as per cash book Rs. 12,840

(ii) Following cheques were deposited but not collected so for.

(i) Rs. 550 (ii) Rs. 260 (iii) Rs. 240

(iii) Following cheques issued but were not encashed

(i) Rs. 439 (ii) Rs, 551 (iii) Rs. 1000 and (iv) Rs. 180

iii) Bank charges Rs. 25 were debited by bank

iv) Divided collected by bank Rs. 975.

7. On the 31 March 2006 Bank Pass Book showed a credit balance of Rs. 16,000. Prepare a Bank Reconciliation statement from the following particulars

   1. Cheques issued for Rs. 11,500 of which cheques amounting Rs. 900 have so far been presented for payment.
   2. A cheque for Rs. 800 sent for collection but not collected so far.
   3. A cheque for Rs. 160 which was received was entered in the bank column of the cash book but was omitted to be paid in to the Bank.
   4. Rs. 85 were credited for interest on current a/c by bank.
   5. Bank charges of Rs. 10 debited by bank.

8. Make out a bank Reconciliation statement as on 31st March, 2006 in respect of the bank a/c balance as per pass Book is Rs. 22,097.52 remittances sent to Bank not shown in the Pass Book is Rs. 198.91

   Cheques drawn but not cashed at bank Rs. 27774.59

   Dividend collected by bank directly Rs. 100/-

   Bank met a London pay order for Rs. 223/- advice was issued after 31st March 06

   Interest allowed by bank is Rs. 117.44 and commission deducted Rs. 2.56

   Which were not intimated to party.

9. On 31st December 2005 the pass book of Mr Menon's current account showed a credit balance of Rs. 10,000. Prepare a bank Reconciliation statement with the following information:

   (i) Mr Menon issued a cheque of Rs. 300 on 25th December but this was not presented for payment whereas this was recorded twice in the cash book.

   (ii) A cheque of Rs. 200 drawn on his saving deposits account had been shown as drawn on current a/c

   (iii) A cheque of Rs. 285 issued in 28th December taken in the cash column of the cash book

   (iv) In the pass book Bank charge of Rs. 25 was recorded twice while an other bank charge of Rs. 17 was not recorded in cash book.

10. From the following particulars, prepare bank reconciliation statement as on...

S.No	Particulars	Rs.
1	Bank balance as per pass book Rs. 5936	
2	Cheques issued for Rs. 2300 but not presented for payment of Rs.1800 and a cheque of Rs. 100 was presented for payment next month	
3	A cheque of Rs. 340 was issued, but dishonoured the party had not yet informed of the fact	
4	Cheques deposited for Rs. 1200 cheque, for Rs. 400 collected only in the next month following the deposits. Whereas cheque of Rs. 300 were dishonoured.	
5	Rs. 200 was deposited in bank on 28th of the month but was credited by the bank on 5th of next month.	
	Collection charges debited by bank for Rs. 75.	
6	Bank interest amounted toRs. 125, but it was not considered in the cash book.	
7		

Overdraft

11. From the following particulars, ascertain the bank balance as per pass book of Mr. P Ranga Rao as at February, 28, 2006

   (i) Credit balance at bank as per cash book on 29th Feb, 2006 Rs. 15000

   (ii) Interest charged by the bank update Rs. 50 is recorded in the Pass book only.

   (iii) Two cheques of Rs. 900 and Rs. 1500 were issued but out of them only one cheque of Rs. 900 was presented for payment up-to-date.

   (iv) Charges of Rs. 25 were also recorded only in the pass book.

(v) Dividends on shares Rs. 650 were collected by the bankers directly for which Mr. Rao did not have any information.

(vi) Cheques paid in to the bank Rs. 2500 but cheques of Rs. 1900 were cleared and credited by the bankers upto 28th Feb 2006.

12. From the following particulars, ascertain the bank balance as per pass book of Mr. Keshri as at 31st March 2006

(i) credit balance is per cash book Rs. 38721

(ii) interest charged by bank recorded in pass book only. Rs. 879

(iii) cheques sent for collection for 2,400 but collected so far only for. 1,879

(iv) dividends on shares collected by bankers with no intimation to Mr. Keshri Rs. 850

(v) cheques issued but not presented for payment were Rs. 1850

(vi) the banker had credited Rs. 200 which sum should have been credited to Mrs. Keshri's account.

(vii) Incidental charges debited by bank with no advice Rs. 20

13. From the following particulars, find out the bank balance as per pass book as on 31st Dec 2005 of Mr. Mukherjee.

i) Bank over draft as per cash book Rs. 1,28,850

ii) Cheque deposited per bank statement but not sent to bank Rs. 4,500

iii) Cheque received in cash book but not sent to bank. Rs. 15,000

iv) Premium on Mukherjee L.I.C paid on standing advice Rs. 7,500

v) Customer's cheque returned Cash per Bank statement Rs. 6,000

vi) Cheque issued but dishonoured on technical grand. Rs. 4500

vii) Bills collected by bank directly Rs. 30,000

viii) Cheques sent for collection Rs. 75,000, but collected so far Rs. 74,970

14. From the following particulars prepare a statement showing the balance that would appear in the Pass Book of Sri Haridas as on 31st Dec 06

S.No.	Particulars	Rs.
1.	Over draft as per cash book	6,310
2	Interest on overdraft for 6 months was debited in the pass book	160
3	Bank charges debited in the pass book	30
4	Cheques issued but not presented for payment	1,168
5	Cheques deposited into Bank but not cleared before 31st Decemeber were for	2,170
6	Interest on investment collected by bank and credited in the pass book	1,200

15. Prepare a bank Reconciliation statement from the following particulars.

S.No.	Particulars	Rs.
1	Bank balance as per pass book (Dr.)	1,500
2	Cheques paid into bank but proceeds not yet collected	485
3	Cheques drawn but not yet presented by the bank	800
4	The Banker charged for sundry expenses & commission	15
5	The Banker had allowed Interest	50

16. From the following information, prepare a Bank Reconciliation statement as on 31.3.05 of Alfa & Co. who had an overdraft balance of Rs. 5750.60 as per pass book on that date-

(i) Cheques deposited into Bank but not shown in the pass book Rs. 3,537.30

(ii) Cheques drawn but not cashed at Bank Rs. 2,500,20

(iii) Dividend of Rs. 2,000 collected by Bank directly under the advice of Alfa & Co. was not recorded in the cash book.

(iv) Debit side of cash Book was wrongly over cast by Rs. 500

(v) Cheques amounting Rs. 370 were deposited into bank but it was recorded in the debit side of the pass book

17. From the following particulars prepare a bank Reconciliation statement-

S.No.	Particulars	Rs.
1	Overdraft as per pass book as on 31.12.05	18,880
2	Interest on overdraft (not yet entered in the cash book)	240
3	Bank charges not yet entered in the cash book	60
4	Cheques drawn but not encashed before 31st Dec 05	2,300
5	Cheques paid into the bank but not cleared before 31st Dec 05	4,340
6	A bill receivable (discounted with the bank in November) dishonoured on 31st Dec. 05	1,000

18. Prepare a Bank Reconciliation statement as on 31.12.05 from the following information.

S.No.	Particulars	Rs.
1	Bank overdraft as on 31.12.05 as per pass book	7891.50
2	Cheques issued but not presented for payment	532.25
3	Cheques deposited but collected ofter Jan 2	631.75
4	Debtors directly repaid to the bank information which was received form the bank on 2.1.06	786.00
5	There was a wrong entry is the bank column on the debit side of the cash book column amounting to Rs.	300.00
6.	Dividend received Rs 125 though credited in the pass book before 31.12.05 was recorded in the cash book on 3.1.06.	125

ANSWERS

B. Objective type Questions

1. (i) a (ii) a

2. (1) (ii)

(2) (i)

(3) (iii)

C. Exercises

1.	Balance As per pass book (cr.)	Rs. 12,670
2.	Balance As per pass book (cr.)	Rs 3,440
3.	Balance as per pass book (Dr.)	Rs. 32.50
4.	Balance as per pass book (cr.)	Rs. 3,815
5.	Balance as per pass book (cr.)	Rs.1,83,600
6.	Balance as per pass book (cr.)	Rs. 14,410
7.	Balance as per pass book (cr.)	Rs. 6,285
8.	Balance as per cash book (Dr.)	Rs. 5,370.04
9.	Balance as per cash book (Dr.)	Rs. 9827
10.	Balance as per cash book (Dr.)	Rs. 5470
11.	Overdraft as per pass book (Dr.)	Rs. 13525
12.	Balance as per pass book (overdraft)	Rs. 37,241
13.	Overdraft as per pass book (Dr.)	Rs. 1,18 380
14.	Overdraft balance as per pass book	Rs. 6,302
15.	Overdraft balance as per pass book	Rs. 1,850.00
16.	Overdraft balance as per cash book (cr.)	Rs. 5473.50
17.	Overdraft balance as per pass book (cr.)	Rs. 15,540
18.	Overdraft balance as per pass book	Rs. 8,403

CHAPTER 8

TRIAL BALANCE AND ERRORS AND THEIR RECTIFICATION

A. Essay Type Questions

1. What is a Trial Balance? Name the errors that are disclosed by Trial Balance.
2. What is Trial Balance? It is true to say that results are accurate if Trial Balance tallies?
3. What do you mean by a Trial Balance? Discuss its main objects & show how it is prepared.
   [Delhi B.Com (pass) 2002.]
4. Give two examples each of the one sided and doubles sided errors. How are they corrected?
   [Meerut, BBA II Sem 1997]
5. What is Trial Balance ? Explain the errors (i) which are revealed by the Trial Balance and (ii) the errors which are not revealed by the trial balance.
6. Is the agreement of a Trial Balance a conclusive proof of accuracy of ledger accounts? If not, what are the errors which remain undetected by the Trial balance?
7. Errors which do not affect the agreement of a trial balance.
   [Delhi B.com (Pass) 2001]
8. Distinguish between -
   (a) Balance Sheet and a Trial Balance
   [Delhi B.Com (pass) 99, 2000, 2003 & 2005]
   (b) Errors of commission and errors of omission.
   [Delhi B.Com (pass) 2000, 2003]
9. Write short notes on the following:
   (i) Error of Principle
   (ii) Compensatory errors
   (iii) Factors affecting disagreement of Trial Balance.

B. Objective Type Questions

1. Indicate to which account should be debited/credited

(i) The amount spent on repairs of an old machinery should be debited to
   (a) Machinery account
   (b) Repairs account
   (c) Cash account
   (d) None of the above.

(ii) The amount spent on purchase of a plant should be debited to
   (a) Purchases a/c
   (b) Plant a/c
   (c) Sales a/c
   (d) None of the above.

(iii) The amount received on sale of a furniture should be credited to
   (a) Sales a/c
   (b) Furniture a/c

(c) Cash a/c
(d) None on the above.

(iv) Goods worth Rs. 200 given away as charity should be credited to
(a) Sales a/c
(b) Purchases a/c
(c) Charity a/c
(d) None of the above.

(v) Goods worth Rs. 500 taken by the proprietor should be credited to
(a) Proprietor's a/c
(b) Sales a/c
(c) Purchases a/c
(d) Drawing a/c

2. Indicate the type of error in the following cases:

(i) Purchases Day Book undercast by Rs. 200.
(a) Error of principle
(b) Compensating Error
(c) Error of Omission
(d) Error of Commission.

(ii) Amount spent on the repair of a plant is wrongly debited to repairs a/c.
(a) Error of Omission
(b) Error of Commission
(c) Error of Principle
(d) Compensating Error.

(iii) Mr. Ram's account is debited in place of Shyam's a/c for Rs. 500.
(a) Error of Omission
(b) Error of Principle
(c) Error of Commission
(d) Compensating Error.

(iv) Sales day book overcast by Rs. 150.
(a) Error of Omission
(b) Error of Commission
(c) Compensation Error
(d) Error of principle.

(v) Purchase of Furniture is debited to Purchases a/c.
(a) Error of Omission
(b) Error of Principle
(c) Error of Commission
(d) None of the above.

(vi) Bad debts recovered from a debtor is credited to his account.
(a) Error of Omission
(b) Error of Commission
(c) Error of Principle
(d) Compensating Error.

C. Exercises

1. Prepare trial balance from the following balances extracted from the books of Mr. Ram Reddy for the year ended on 30.06.2006

	Rs.		Rs.
Capital	25000	Purchases	62000
Debtors	20000	Sales	73020
Creditors	14000	Sales Returns	600
Drawings	4200	Wages	9000
Opening Stock	12000	General Expenses	3500
Bad debts	1720	Bank Overdraft	2900
Furniture	4000	provision for Bad debts	2100

2. Indicate in which side the following items would appear in a Trial Balance - Capital a/c, Drawing a/c, Debtors a/c, Creditors a/c, Outstanding expenses, Prepaid expenses, Accrued incomes, Unaccrued incomes, salaries paid, rent paid, discount allowed, discount received, returns inward, returns outwards, Bills payable, Bills receivable, bank overdraft, cash in hand, cash at bank, Land and buildings, Plant and Machinery, furniture and fixture, Good will a/c., discount on issue of shares a/c and preliminary expenses a/c.

3. From the following balances extracted from the books of Mr. Rama Rao, prepare a trial balance for the year ended on 31. 12-2005.

	Rs.		Rs.
Opening stock	9.950	Share Capital	20.000
Purchases	54,525	Debtors	8,000
Sales	85.000	Creditors	10000
Carriage Inwards	1.425	Bank overdraft	3.900
Indirect expenses	19.500	Land & building	15.000
Loss on sale of an asset	400	Plant	8.000
Profit on sale of investment	600	Cash at hand	3000
Interest on Investment	300		

4. The following balances are extracted from the books of Mr. Rakesh as on 31.12.2005

	Rs.		*Rs.*
Capital	15,000	Purchases	7 ,200
Land & Building	15,600	Provision for bad debts	370
Bank overdraft	2,500	Sales	17,000
Cash in hand	680	Wages	1250
Stock in Trade as on 1.1.04	6,000	Salaries	700
Advertisement	210	Insurance	40
Rent & Taxes	160	Discount allowed	300
Interest & Discount received	300	Repairs to building	210
Debtors	6420	Creditors	4,100
		General Expenses	500

Prepare a trial balance

5. Give the journal entries necessary to rectify the following errors :
   (i) A payment of Rs. 250 for purchase of a Typewriter for office use has been debited to Purchases a/c.
   (ii) A credit sale of Rs. 127 to Mr. Chandra has been posted to the debit of Mr. Kuchhal's account from the Sales Day book.
   (iii) A payment of Rs. 96 for white washing the office has been charged to Buildings accounts.

6. Rectify the following Errors :

(i) Sales to Vinod Rs. 143 posted to his account as Rs. 134.

(ii) Sales to Vinod Rs. 143 debited to his account as Rs. 134.

(iii) Sales to Vinod Rs. 143 credited to his account as Rs. 134.

7. Rectify the following Errors :

(i) Wages paid for the construction of office debited to wages account Rs. 1,500.

(ii) Cartage paid for the newly purchased furniture Rs. 10 posted to cartage account.

(iii) Furniture purchased on credit from Ram for Rs. 300 posted as Rs. 30.

(iv) Sales to X Rs. 400 posted to Y's account.

(v) Wages paid Rs. 2,550 were recorded in the cash book as Rs. 2,505.

(vi) Purchases from Y Rs. 1,002 were omitted from the books.

8. Rectify any three of the following by passing journal entries :

(i) A machine of Rs. 500 purchased for cash from B has been passed through the purchases Book.

(ii) Sales of Rs. 5,000 to A has been posted to the credit of his account at Rs. 500.

(iii) Insurance Premium of Rs. 350 paid on the private property of the proprietor has been charged to the Insurance Premium a/c.

(iv) Repairs to an old machine Rs. 250, the payment for a new machine Rs. 7,000 and the freight of Rs. 75 paid on the new machine have all been debited to Machinery account.

(v) A bill received from C for repairs to an old fan Rs. 25 and for the supply of a cooler by him for Rs. 450 have been entered in the Invoice book.

9. Pass Journal entries to rectify the following errors :

(i) A purchase amounting to Rs. 1000 made for a staff member, was recorded in the purchases book.

(ii) Wages paid to workers for installing a machinery Rs. 750, were debited to wages account.

(iii) A dishonored bill receivable for Rs. 5000 returned by the bank with whom it had been discounted was credited to bank and debited to bills receivable account.

(iv) A sum of Rs. 1000 drawn by the proprietor for his personal use was debited to travelling expenses account.

10. Ganesh drew a trial balance of his operations for the year ended 31.03.2006. There was a difference in the trial balance which he closed with a suspense account. On scrutiny by the auditors, the following errors were found.

(i) Purchases day book for the month of April 05 was under cast by Rs. 1000.

(ii) Sales Day book of October, 05 was overcast by Rs. 10,000.

(iii) A furniture purchased for Rs. 8100 was entered in the furniture a/c as Rs. 810.

(iv) A bill for Rs. 10,000 drawn by Ganesh was not entered in the bills receivable book.

(v) A machinery purchased for Rs. 10,000 was entered in the purchases day book.

Pass necessary journal entries to rectify the same and ascertain the difference in the trial balance that was shown under the suspense account in respect of the above items.

11. There was difference in the trial balance of Sri Arihant which was put to a newly opened suspense account. Subsequently the following mistakes were discovered. Pass journal entries to rectify them and ascertain the difference in the trial balance.

(i) Materials Costing Rs. 1700 in the erection of the machinery and the wages for it amounting to Rs. 1,400 were included in the purchases account and the wage account respectively.

(ii) Goods sold under credit terms Rs. 16,900 to music were recorded properly in the sales book but were debited to his account as Rs. 19600 and carriage outward and freight paid Rs. 700 chargeable from him were posted to sales expenses account.

(iii) Sales return by Yogeshwar Rs. 2300 were correctly recorded in the sales return book from where they were debited to Yogeshwar's account by Rs. 32.

(iv) Old furniture originally purchased for Rs. 1800 written down to Rs. 1100 was sold for Rs. 1700 and was credited to furniture account.

(v) Machinery purchased on credit Rs. 17000 was recorded in purchases book and transport charges for the machine Rs. 1200 were debited to trade expenses account.

12. Rectify the following errors by passing necessary journal entries.

(i) Goods taken by the proprietor Rs. 1500 for gift to his daughter were not recorded at all.

(ii) Rs. 1500 received from Praveen against debts previously written off as bad debits have been credited to his personal account.

(iii) Received interest Rs. 150, posted to loan account.

(iv) A cheque received from Amar, a debtor for Rs. 2000, was directly received by the proprietor who deposited it in to his personal account.

13. The books of accounts of B. Quick for the year ending 31st March 2006 were closed with a difference in books carried forward. The following errors were detected subsequently :

(i) Goods Rs. 125 returned to Mitra Bros were recorded in the returns inward book as Rs. 250 and there from it was posted to the debit of Mitra Bros. Account.

(ii) A credit sale of Rs. 760 was wrongly posted as Rs. 670 to the customer's account in the sales ledger.

(iii) Closing stock was overstated by Rs. 5000 being casting error in the schedule of inventory.

(iv) Paid acceptance to Bala Ram for Rs. 7600 was posted to the debit of Sita Ram as Rs. 6700.

(v) Goods purchased from Rs. 3250 entered in the sales Day book for Rs. 3520.

(vi) Rs. 1500 being the total of the discount column on the credit side of the cash book was not posted. Pass necessary rectification entries.

14. While preparing the final accounts for the year ended 31st March 2006, Mr. Smart could not get his trial balance agreed. He transferred the difference to suspense account. In April 2006, the following errors were discovered in the books of account.

(i) The sales book for January 2006 was undercast by Rs. 1000.

(ii) Entertainment expenses Rs. 150 incurred in February 04 were omitted to be posted from the cash book to the ledger.

(iii) Discount column on the receipt side of the cash book for February 2006 was added as Rs. 2230 instead of Rs. 2130.

(iv) A purchase from Mr. Sumer for Rs. 8200 on March 5, 2006 was recorded correctly in the purchases book but the supplier was wrongly debited for the purchase.

Pass the necessary journal entries to rectify the above mentioned errors. Also prepare (a) suspense account and (b) profit and loss adjustment account.

B. Objective Type Questions

1. Indicate to which account should be debited/credited

(i) (a) (ii) (b) (iii) (b) (iv) (b) (v) (c)

2. Indicate the Type of Error

(i) (d) (ii) (c) (iii) (d) (iv) (b) (v) (b) (vi) (b)

C. Exercises

1. Total of trial balance Rs. 1,17.020
3. Total of trial balance Rs. 1,19.800
4. Total of Trial Balance Rs. 39,270
10. Difference in trial balance Rs. 18290
11. Total of suspense a/c Rs. 8,200
14. Total of suspense a/c Rs. 17.500

CHAPTER 9

DEPRECIATION – RESERVES AND PROVISIONS

A. Essay Type Questions

1. Explain the nature and need of Depreciation.
2. Define depreciation. Explain its rationale. What are different methods of calculating depreciation?
Meerut, B.BA II Sec. 1997]
3. What is depreciation? What is the need for providing depreciation? Describe two methods of providing depreciation. Also explain the effects of depreciation on:
   (a) Profit and loss account, and
   (b) The Balance Sheet
4. What is depreciation and how it is caused? Distinguish between the straight line Method and the written down value method of depreciation of capital assets. [Delhi B.Com (Pass) 2001 (B), 2005]
5. What do you understand by Depreciation Discuss version methods of providing depreciation with illustration.
6. Distinguish between straight line method and Diminishing balance method of depreciation.
Delhi B.Com (Pass) 2002, 2005]
7. Define Depreciation, Depletion and amortization.
8. Discuss the merits and demerits of sinking Fund Method of Depreciation.
[Delhi B.Com (Pas) 1994(B), 2005]
9. State the merits and demerits of annuity method of depreciation.
[Delhi B.Com (Pas) 2000]
10. Distinguish between Sinking Fund to repay liability and Depreciation Fund to replace wasty asset.
[Delhi. B.Com (Pass) 1998]

12. What is general reserve? How it is different from capital reserve?
[Delhi B.Com (Pass) 2000]
13. What is secret reserve? How is it ??? Explain its merits and demerits.
14. Distinction between Annuity method and depreciation fund method.
[Delhi, B. Com(pass), 2002(B)]
15. Describe (i) The points of similarity and (ii) points of distinction between depreciation fund method and Insurance policy method of providing depreciation.
[Delhi, B.Com (pass) 1999 B]

B. Objective Type Questions

1. Indicate which one is correct in the following cases-
   (a) Depreciation is calculated on the basis of
      (i) cost price
      (ii) Market price
      (iii) Cost or market price which ever is less
      (iv) None of the above.

(b) Reserve is created-
  (i) to meet out future contingencies
  (ii) to strengthen the financial position of the business
  (iii) to meet out any liability
  (iv) None of the above.

(c) Provision is-
  (i) an appropriation of profit.
  (ii) A charge against the profit
  (iii) A surplus
  (iv) None of the above.

(d) Amount of depreciation if charged on the basis of straight line method
  (i) increases every year
  (ii) decreases every year
  (iii) remains constant

(e) Amount of depreciation if charged on the basis of written down value method
  (i) Increases every year
  (ii) remains constant
  (iii) decreases every year

C. Exercises

1. Rakesh purchased a Machine for Rs. 12,000. The expected life of machine is 4 years. If its scrap realizes Rs 1,200. Calculate the amount of depreciation to be charged from profit and loss a/c for 4 years. Prepare machine account of all the 4 years under straight line method of charging depreciation.

2. Golden Transport Company, New Delhi purchased 3 Trucks it Rs. 4,00,000 each on 1st Jan 2003 from the dealer. The company decided to charge 20% deprecation on the basis of original cost of trucks.

   Prepare Trucks A/c for 3 years and find out its w.d.v. at the end of 3rd year.

3. M/s X and Y purchased a machine (second hand) for Rs. 8000 on 18 April, 2002. They spent Rs. 3,500 on its overhand and installation. Depreciation is written of @ 10% on the purchased cost. On 30 June 2005, it was found to be unsuitable and sold for Rs. 6500.

   Prepare Machine a/c from 2002 to 2005 assuming that account books are closed on 31st December.

4. A purchased a second hand machine for Rs. 40,000 it was over hauled and installed on 1.1.2002 installation charges being Rs. 10,000. On 1.7.2002 another machine was purchased for Rs. 20,000. On 1.7.2004 the plant installed on 1.1.2002 was sold for Rs. 25,000, dismantling charge being Rs. 1.000. On the same date, another machine was purchased for Rs. 80,000 which was commissioned on 30.9.04. Accounts are closed on 31st December. Depreciation is charged @ 10% p.a. on original cost. Show plant account for 4 years.

5. On 1st October 2002 M/s Goyal Traders, installed one machine in their shop at a total cost of Rs. 1;50,000. On 1st April, 2004 another machine of the cost of Rs. 50,000 was installed. Depreciation is charged depreciation at 10% p.a. on the reduced balances every year. Accounts are closed on every 31st March.

   Prepare Machine Account for first three years.

6. On 1.2003 M/s K.K. traders of Rajasthan purchased plants amounted to Rs. 2,00,000 and decided to write off depreciation @ 25% on written down value method. Show the plants a/c for first three years.

7. Thaper oil and fats limited purchased furniture for the office amounting to Rs. 12,500. The company wanted to charge depreciation @ 10% p.a.

   Prepare Furniture a/c for three years when

(a) Depreciation is charged on original cost method and

(b) When it is charged on reducing balance method.

8. On 1st April, 2004 Rakesh purchased a machine for Rs. 8000. The life of the machine was expected to be four years. It was decided to write off 90% of the original cost over the life time setting aside equal sum on the annual closing date of 31st March.

   Prepare Machine account for the year 2004-05.

9. Calculate the amount of depreciation to be charged from profit and loss a/c from the following information.

	Rs.
Cost of machine	1,00,000
Estimated residual value	5,000
Life of the assets	10 years

10. Mr. Ajay purchased a machine from Mayank on 1st Jan 2003 for Rs. 60,000 and spent Rs. 4000 on its erection/installation. The firm writes off depreciation @15% of the original cost of the machine.

    Prepare machinery account for two years assuming that the books are closed on 31st December every year.

11. Mr. Prasad purchased a machine on 1st April 2003 for Rs. 40,000. It is depreciated 10% per annum on the original cost of the machine. On 30th Sep 05 it is sold for Rs. 25,000.

    Prepare machinery account assuming that the books are closed on 31st December every year.

12. Mr. John purchased a second hand plant for Rs. 28,000 and spent Rs. 2000 on its repairs. On 1.1.2002 the buyer decide to charge depreciation @ 10%. On reducing balance method. On 1.7.2003 another machine for Rs. 10,000 was purchased.

    Prepare machine account for 3 years assuming that books are closed on 31st December each year.

13. Mr. Ali purchased a machine on 1st April 2002 for Rs. 50,000. Another machine was purchased on 1st October 2003 for Rs. 10.000. On 1st July 04 a part of the machine valued Rs. 20,000 purchased on 1.4.02 is disposed off for Rs. 9,000 and another machine on the same date is purchased for Rs. 12,000.

    Prepare machinery account for 4 years assuming (1) Accounts are closed on 31st December each year and (2) The firm charges 20% per annum depreciation on written down value.

14. Mr. Sachin purchased on 1st January 2002 certain machinery for Rs. 58,000 and spent Rs. 2000 on its erection. On 1st July, 2002 additional Machinery costing Rs. 30,000 was purchased. On 1st July 2004, the machinery purchased on 1st January 2002 having become obsolete was auctioned for Rs. 32,000. On the same date fresh machinery was purchased at a cost of Rs. 50000.

    Depreciation was provided annually on 31st December at the rate of 10% on reducing balance method.

    Give machinery account as it would appear at the end of year from 2002 to 2004.

15. Kaushal Traders purchased a second hand machinery an 1st Jan 2005 for Rs. 2,3000 and spent Rs. 2000 on its repair. It was decided to depreciate the machinery @20% p.a. on 31st December at diminishing balance Method.

    Prepare the machinery account from 2003 to 2005 and show profit or loss as it was sold on 31st December 2005 for Rs. 10,800.

16. A boiler was purchased from abroad for Rs. 10000 shipping and forward charges amounted to Rs. 2000, import duty Rs. 7000 and expenses of installation amounted in Rs. 1000.

    Calculate depreciation for the first three years. (separately for each year) @ 10% on diminishing balance method.

17. A company had bought machinery for Rs. 2,00,000 including a boiler with Rs. 20,000. The machinery account had been credited for depreciation on reducing instalment system for the past four years at the rate of 10%. During the fifth i.e. the present year, the boiler becomes useless on account of damage to some of its vital parts. The damaged boiler is sold for Rs. 4000. Write up the machinery account.

18. The original cost of furniture amounted to Rs. 1000 and it is decided to write off 5% on the original cost as depreciation at the end of each year. Show the ledger account as it will appear during first four years. Also show how the same account will appear if it was decided to write off 5% on the diminishing balance.

19. On 1st January 2002, machinery was purchased for Rs. 20000. On 1st July 2003 another machine was purchased for Rs. 10,000 and on 1 January 2004 one more machine was purchased for Rs. 5000. The firm depreciates its machinery @ 20% on the diminishing balance method. Show the machine for four year.

20. On 1st January 2001, a merchant purchased a furniture costing Rs. 55000. It is estimated that its working life is 10 year at the end of which it will fetch Rs. 5000. Additions are made on 1st Jan. 2002 and 1st July 2004 to the value of Rs. 9500 and Rs. 8,400 (Residual values Rs. 500 and Rs. 400 respectively)

Show furniture a/c for the first four years, if depreciation is written off according to the straight line method.

21. A company whose accounting year is the calendar year, purchased machineries 1st April, 2001 costing Rs. 30,000.

It further purchased a machine costing Rs. 20,000 on 1st October 2001 and another machine costing Rs. 10,000 on 1st July 2002.

On 1st January 2003 of the machineries which were purchased on 1st April, 2001 one machine costing Rs. 10,000 became obsolete and was sold for Rs. 3000.

Show how the machinery account would appear for all the 3 years in the books of the company after charging depreciation @ 10% p.a. on written down value method.

22. A company purchased machine for Rs. 15,000 on 1st April, 2000. Additional machinery was acquired for Rs. 40000 on 31st Sep. 2001 and for Rs. 25,000 on 1st April, 2003. Certain machinery, which was purchased for Rs. 40000 on 31st Sep. 2001 was sold for Rs. 300,000 on 30 Sep, 2003.

Give the machinery account for the year ending 31st March 2004 taking into account

(1) That the depreciation charged @ 10% on W.D.V. and

(2) Firm closes its book on 31st March every year.

23. ABC and Co. closes its accounts on 31st March every year. On 1.7.2001 machineries costing Rs. 60,000 were purchased. Further on 1.1.2002 a machinery costing Rs. 60,000 was purchased and another machine costing Rs. 10000 on 1.10.2002 was also taken.

Out of machineries which were purchased on 1.7.2001, one machine costing Rs. 20,000 became obsolete and was sold for Rs. 6000 on 1.4.2003.

On 1.1.2004, a new machine was purchased for Rs. 30,000.

Show how the machinery account would appear for all the three years in the books of the Co. after charging depreciation @ $33\frac{1}{3}\%$ on written down value method. While preparing the machinery account, you are required to observe the following notes-

(i) Calculate the amount of depreciation to the nearest rupee.

(ii) Provide depreciation for the full year even if the machinery has been used for a part of the year.

24. On 1.1.2000 A purchased roasting machine for Rs. 60,000 and Grinding machine for Rs. 40,000. On 1.1.2001 he purchased one oil expeller for Rs. 1,00,000. On 1.1.02 the roasting machine got out of order and a new roaster was purchased costing Rs. 1,20,000 after surrendering the old one and paying cash Rs. 90,000. On 1.1.2003 the oil expeller purchased on 1.1.01 was destroyed by fire and the insurance co. paid Rs. 60,000 only.

Show the machinery account for 2000, 2001, 2002, and 2003 charging depreciation @ 10% p.a. on the W.D.V. method.

25. Gopal Oil Mills on 1.1.2002 purchased a plant for Rs. 1,00,000 Depreciation was provided at 10% per annum on original cost annually on 31st December. With effect from 1.1.2004, the company decided

to change the method of depreciation to written down value, the rate of depreciation being 15% per annum.

Prepare plant account for three years i.e. from 2002 to 2004.

26. A machine was purchased on 1st January, 2001 for Rs 19,400 and Rs. 600 on spent on its erections were 1st July in the same year, additional machinery costing Rs. 10,000 was acquired. On 1st July 2003 further additional machinery was purchased at a cost of Rs. 15,000

Depreciation was provided annually on 31st December at the rate of 10% per annum on the original cost of the asset. In 2004, however, the method was changed to one of writing off 15% per annum on written down value as on January 1, 2004.

Give the machinery account as it would stand at the end of each year from 2001 to 2004. Make your calculation for the nearest rupee. [Delhi B. Com (Hons) I year 2004] modified (figures 10 times).

27. M/S Goyal Traders purchased on 1st January 2002, a second hand machinery for Rs. 28,000 and spent Rs. 2000 on its repairs. On 1st April 2003, additional machinery costing Rs. 20,000 was purchased. On 1st July 2004, the machinery purchased on 1st January, 2002 became obsolete and was sold off for Rs. 20,000. Depreciation was provided annually on 31st December @ 10% per annum on the original cost of the asset. In 2004, however, the trader changed this method of providing depreciation and adopted the method of writing off 15% on written down value.

Show the machinery account from the year 2002 to 2004.

28. MGF purchased a second hand machinery on 1st January 2002 for Rs. 37000 and immediately spent Rs. 2000 on its repairs and Rs. 1000 on its erection. On 1st July 2003, it purchased another machine for Rs. 10.000 and on 1st July 2004 sold off the first machine purchased in 2002 for Rs. 28,000, on the same date, it purchased a machinery for Rs. 25,000. On 1st July 2005 the second machinery purchased for Rs. 10000 was sold off for Rs. 2000.

Depreciation was provided on the machinery at a rate of 10% on the original cost annually on 31st December, 2005, however, the company changed the method of providing depreciation and adopted the written down value method, the rate of depreciation being 15%.

Give the machinery account for four years commencing from January 1,2002.

Calculations are to be made to the nearest rupee.

29. A second hand machinery was purchased on 1st January 2001 for Rs. 30,000, Rs. 6000 and Rs. 4000 were spent on its repairs and erection respectively on the same date. On 1st July, 2002 another machine was purchased for Rs. 26000 and on 1st July, 2003 the first machinery having become obsolete was auctioned for Rs. 30,000. On the same date another machinery was purchased for Rs. 25,000. On 1st July, 2004 the second hand machinery was also sold off and it fetched Rs. 23,000. Depreciation was provided on Machinery @ 10% p.a. on the original cost on 31st December. In 2003, the method of providing depreciation was changed to the written down value method, the rate of depreciation being 15%. Prepare machinery account from 2001 to 2004.

ANSWERS

B. Objective Type Questions

(a) (i)

(b) (ii)

(c) (ii)

(d) (iii)

(e) (iii)

C. Exercises

1.		Amount of Depreciation	Rs. 2,700
2.		Balance of trucks a/c	Rs. 4,80,000
3.		Loss on sale of machine	Rs. 1262.50
4.		Balance of Plant a/c	Rs. 81,000
5.		Closing Balance of Machine	Rs. 1,60,425
6.		Balance of Machine a/c	Rs. 96,000
7.		Balance of Machine a/c	Rs. 9,112.50
8.		Annual Sum	Rs. 1,800
9.		Amount of Depreciation	Rs. 9,500
10.		Balance of Machine	Rs. 44,800
11.		Loss on Sale	Rs. 5.000
12.		Balance of Machine a/c	Rs. 30,420
13.	(i)	Loss on Sale	Rs. 3240
	(ii)	Balance of Machine a/c	Rs. 27,776
14.	(i)	Loss on Sale	Rs. 14,170
	(ii)	Balance of Machine a/d	Rs. 70585
15.		Loss on Sale	Rs. 2,000
16.		Balance of builder a/c	Rs. 14,580
17.	(a)	Loss on Sale	Rs. 9,122
	(b)	Balance of Machine a/c	Rs. 1,06,258
18.	(a)	Balance of Furniture	Rs. 3,200
	(b)	Balance of furniture	Rs. 3257.50
19.		Balance of Machine a/c	Rs. 27,630
20		Balance of furniture a/c	Rs. 49,800
21.	(a)	Loss on Sale	Rs. 5,325
	(b)	Balance of Machine a/c	Rs. 39,330
22.	(a)	Profit on Sale	Rs. 1,510
	(b)	Balance of Machinery a/c	Rs. 1,20,915
23.	(a)	Loss on Sale	Rs. 2889
	(b)	Balance of Machine a/c	Rs. 54074
24.	(a)	Loss on Sale	Rs. 21,000
	(b)	Balance of Machine a/c	Rs. 1,23,444
25.		Balance of Machine a/c	Rs. 68,000
26.		Balance of Machine a/c	Rs. 25.830
27.	(a)	Loss on Sale	Rs. 2500
	(b)	Balance of machinery a/c	Rs. 15,725
28.	(a)	Loss on Sale of I Machine	Rs. 2000
	(b)	Loss on sale of II Machine	Rs. 5862.50
	(c)	Balance of Machinery	Rs. 20,087.50
29.	(a)	Profit on Sale	Rs. 3580
	(b)	Balance of machinery	Rs. 19,656

CHAPTER 10

BILLS OF EXCHANGE

A. Essay Type Questions

1. What is a Bill of exchange? Distinguish between a Bill of Exchange and a Promissory Note.
2. What are the types of bills? Explain the advantages of using bills.
3. What do you mean by renewal of a bill? How will you deal with interest in case of renewal of a bill?
4. What is Days of Grace? How is the date of maturity calculated? Illustrate.
5. What do you mean by accommodation bill? Distinguish between Trade bill and an accommodating bill.

B. Objective Type Questions

1. Indicate the correct one from the following:

(A) A bill of Exchange has the following No. of parties

(i) One (ii) Two

(iii) Three (iv) Four.

(B) A Promissory Note has the following No. of parties

(i) One (ii) Two

(iii) Three (iv) None of the above

(c) Dishonour of a bill means

(i) Full payment on the expiry of period (ii) No payment on the expiry of period

(iii) If bill is endorsed in favour of other party (iv) None of the above

(D) Days of Grace is of

(i) One Day (ii) two days

(iii) Three days (iv) Not known

(E) What is the date of maturity if a bill is accepted on the 4th Feb. for two months:

(i) 4th April (ii) 4th May

(iii) 7th April (iv) 7th May

(F) Retiring of a bill means

(i) Payment on due date (ii) Payment before due date

(iii) No payment (iv) Payments as and when funds are available

(G) Bill of Exchange is drawn by

(i) a debtor (ii) a creditor

(iii) a bank (iv) None of the above

(H) The entry regarding payment of bill will be passed in the books of drawer if the bill is

(i) retained by the drawer (ii) is encashed/discounted

(iii) is endorsed and (iv) retained and sent for collection to the banker

(I) If a bill is dishonoured for Rs. 2,000, noting charges paid are Rs. 50 and the bank charges Rs. 20 as interest, what would be the amount for the renewable of a bill.

(i) Rs. 2000 (ii) Rs. 2020

(iii) Rs. 2070 (iv) Rs. 2050

2. Do you agree with the following statement?

(i) Payment of the bill before maturity is a retiring a bill under Rebate.

(ii) Full payment can be realized only after the insolvency of the drawee.

(iii) Noting charges is a gain for the drawee.

C. Exercises

1. Before the maturity date of the bill for Rs. 300,

   (a) X, the acceptor approached us and pays Rs. 100 in cash and ask us to draw on him another bill for Rs. 215. Rs. 15 being for interest and we agree to it.

   (b) X pays Rs. 115 and accepts another bill for Rs. 200

   (c) X pays us Rs. 25 for interest and we draw another bill for the full amount.

   (d) X pays us Rs. 100 in cash and endorses over to us a bilk for Rs. 75 and we draw on him a fresh bill for the balance plus Rs. 20 for interest.

   Pass necessary journal entries to record the above transactions

2. Shri G. sold his diamond ring to Shri K. for RS. 20,000 and received a bill of exchange for three months of the amount. There after. Shri G. discounted the bill with his bankers receiving Rs. 19,800. Shri K. was not able to meet the bill on the due date. Shri K, however, agreed to accept a new 3 months bill for the amount due by him together with interest @ 9% p.a. and discount charges.

   Show the journal entries and ledger account in the books of Shri G. and Shri K.

3. Karun draws a bill for Rs. 2000 on Tarun, Tarun accepts the bill and returns it to Karun on the same date. Karun endorses it to Barun who passes it out to Alok. The latter discounts the bill for Rs. 1950. The bill is finally dishonoured.

   Give the entries in the books all parties, i.e. Karun, Tarun, Barun and Alok.

4. 1st July 2006 M owes to S Rs. 1200 and accepts three bills of Rs. 400 each due respectively in one, two and four months. The first bill is retained by S. and is duly met. The second bill was discounted (charges being Rs. 4) and is met in due course. The third bill is also discounted (charges being Rs. 4) and is dishonoured. The noting charges being Rs. 10.

   New arrangements are duly made whereby M Pays cash Rs.100 and accepts a bill due in two months for the balance of the amount with interest at 6% per annum. The bill is retained. On due date the same is dishonoured, notational charges being Rs. 7. M shortly became insolvent and 25 paise in the rupee was received from his estate. Pass Journal entries in the books of S.

5. Enter the following transactions in the Bill Receivable Book of N. Bhagwan:

   Feb 1. Drew of Gopikishan at 30 days sight Rs. 10,000 against sales.

   Feb 2. Drew on Ramanlal at 45 days sight; Rs. 15,750 against sales. Drew on Gopikishan at 30 days sight; Rs. 14,200 against sales.

   Feb 3. Drew on Ramanlal at 45 days sight; Rs. 16,000 against sales. On the 4th February all the above bills were discounted by Bhagwan with his Bank, the discount rates being:

   (a) Rs. 15 per thousand in the case of 30 days bills; and

   (b) Rs. 22.50 per thousand in the case of 45 days bills.

   Fraction thousand are treated as a thousand for discount rate purpose.Show also the entries in the books of Bhagwan in:

   (i) The Bills Receivable A/c

   (ii) Gopikishan A/c and Ramanlal A/c

6. On 1.1.2006...; R supplied goods to P to the value ofRs. 9,000 and settled the account by means of three bills of exchange for Rs. 3,000 each, due respectively after two, three and four months. A week later R discounted the first bill with his banker at a discount of Rs. 60, he held the other bills.

   The first two bills were paid at maturity. On the date of maturity of the third bill, P arranged to renew the bill paying Rs. 1,000 in cash and giving R a fresh bill for four months to cover the balance with interest @ 6% p.a. R discounted the bill for Rs. 1920 and the bill was paid on maturity. Show the entries in the books of both the parties.

7. Sen and Banerjee have a number of transactions on bill of exchange between them. You are required to show the Journal entries in their books in respect of the following transactions.

1.1.2006 Sen draws a bill on Banerjee for Rs. 15,450 payable after one month, inclusive of interest at 3 per cent per month.

3.1.2006 Sen discounts a bill for Rs. 25,000 drawn on 30-12-1997 with his Bank, charges being 15 per cent per annum. The bill is payable on 3-2-1979.

4-1-2006 Sen endorses the bill for Rs. 15,450 in favour of R.Ram towards accounts.

1-2-2006 Banerjee pays the bill for Rs. 15,450.

4-2-2006 The bill for Rs. 25,000 is returned by sen's bankers as unpaid with their charged of Rs.10.

8. On the 1st January 2006 Bimal draw on Chetan three bills of exchange in full settlement of Claims, the first for Rs. 14,000 at one months; and the second for Rs. 16,000 at two months and the third for Rs. 18,000 at three months. The bills were duly accepted by Chetan.

The first bill was endorsed by Bimal to his creditor Tarun on 3rd January, 2006 the second bill was discounted on 15th January 2006 for Rs. 15,900 and the third bill was sent to bank for collection on 4th February, 2006. All the bills were duly met on maturity except the second bill which was dishonored, noting charges being Rs. 240. Bimal charged Chetan Rs. 300 for interest and drew on him a fourth bill for two months for the amount due. The fourth bill was duly met on maturity.

Pass the Journal Entries (including narration) in the books of Bimal.

9. Mitra, for the mutual accommodation of himself and Ghosh draws upon the latter bill of exchange at 3 months for Rs. 6,000 dated 1.1.06 Mitra discounts the bill immediately at his banker, the rate of discount being 5% and hands ever half of the proceed to Ghosh.

Ghosh for a similar purpose and at the same time, draws a bill at 3 months for Rs. 3,000. Thus he discounts at his banker at 5% and hands over half the proceeds to Mitra. Ghosh becomes bankrupt on 31st March 2006 and a first and final dividend of 25 paise in the rupee is paid on his estate on 30.6.1998.

Write up Ghosh's Account in Mitra's book. Assume in each case that one-half of the charge for discounting the bill is chargeable to Ghosh and one-half to Mitra.

10. For their mutual accommodation K.Kamat accepted on 1.3.2006 a bill drawn on him by R.Ratnam for Rs. 4,000 for three months. This bill was discounted for Rs. 90 discount and the money was sent by Ratam to Kamat.

On the same day, and for the same purpose Kamat received an acceptance from Ratnam for Rs. 6,000 for three months. This bill was discounted for Rs. 90 discount and the proceeds were shared as two-third to Kamat and one-third to Ratnam.

Before the due date, Kamat sent a cheque to Ratnam in full settlement of his account, but at maturity Ratnam became insolvent and his estate paid a dividend of 50 paise in the rupee. Give the journal entries in the books of K. Kamat and R. Ratnam.

11. Journalise the following bill transactions in the books of K.Katrak:

(i) Katrak's acceptance to B.Basu for Rs. 2,000 and an acceptance of new bill for the balance plus Rs. 10, for interest.

(ii) G.Gupta's acceptance for Rs. 4,000 which was endorsed over by Katrak to M. Mehta was dishonoured, Mehta paid Rs. 20 noting charges.

(iii) D.Dulal retires a bill for Rs. 2,000 drawn on him by Kartrak for Rs. 10 discount.

(iv) Katrak's acceptance to P.Patel for Rs. 5,000 discharged by M.Mody's acceptance to Katrak for a similar amount.

12. A, B and C for mutual accommodation drew the following bills all for three months:

A drew on B for Rs. 15,000 and on C Rs. 12,000

B drew on A for Rs. 18,000 and on C Rs. 30,000

C drew on A for Rs. 24,000 and on B Rs. 12,000

All the bills were discounted at 10% and were shared equally. On due date C became insolvent.

Show entries in the books of all the parties assuming that A and B had sent the money due and paid their obligation.

ANSWERS

C. Objective Type questions

1.	(A) (iii)	(B) (ii)	(C) (ii)	(D) (iii)
	(E) (iii)	(F) (ii)	(G) (ii)	
	(H) (i)	(I) (iii)		
2.	(i) Yes	(ii) No	(iii) No.	

CHAPTER 11

FINAL ACCOUNTS OF TRADING CONCERNS

A. Essay Type Questions

1. What is trading account? How far it is different from (a) manufacturing account and (b) profit and loss account.
2. Distinguish between-
   (i) Capital and revenue expenditure

   [Delhi, B.Com.(Pass) 2000, 2002 (B)]

   (ii) Fixed and current assets

   [Delhi B.Com(Pass) 1999 (B), 2002 (B)]

   (iii) Balance Sheet and Trial Balance.

   [Delhi, B. Com (Pass) 1999, 2000, 2003, 2005]

   (iv) Profit and loss a/c and balance sheet.

   (v) Accrued and outstanding income. [Delhi B.Com(Pass) 1996]
3. What do you understand by the grouping and marshalling used in connection with the balance sheet of a company)?

   [Delhi. B.Com. (Pass) 1996]
4. What adjustment are required to close the books of accounts? Explain in detail
5. Write short notes on the following :
   (a) Contingent liabilities [Delhi, B.Com (Pass) 2000, 200 1 (B), 2005]
   (b) Wasting assets. [Delhi, B.Com (Pass) 1999, 2004]
   (c) Intangible assets. [Delhi B.Com (Pass) 2002 (B)]
   (d) Fictitious Assets [Delhi, B. Com. (Pass) 2001]
   (e) Prepaid Expenses [Delhi B.Com (Pass) 2000]
   (f) Accrued/Earned income.
   (g) Unaccrued/unearned income. [Delhi, B.Com. (Pass) 2006 (B)]
   (h) Patent rights

B. Objective Type Questions

(i) Indicate which is the correct answer :

(a) Closing stock is valued at

(ii) cost

(iii) Market price

(iv) Cost or market price whichever is less

(v) None of the above.

(b) goodwill is-

   (i) Tangible asset

   (ii) current asset

   (iii) Intangible asset

   (iv) None of the above.

(c) Discount on the issue of shares/debentures is-
- (i) Revenue expenditure
- (ii) Capital Expenditure
- (iii) Deferred revenue expenditure
- (iv) None of the above

(d) Preliminary expenses are shown in the balance sheet as-
- (i) current assets
- (ii) fixed assets
- (iii) intangible assets.
- (iv) None of the above

(II) State whether the following statements are True and False-

Rent outstanding is a nominal account.

Insurance prepared is a personal account.

Interest received is an asset.

Interest accrued is an asset.

Bad debts is a personal account.

C. Exercises

1. Calculate the Gross Profit from the following :

	Rs.
Opening stock	11,500
Purchases	1,05,000
Wages	3,500
Sales	1,40,000

2. Calculate the cost of materials consumed from the following :

	Rs.
Opening Stock-	
Raw materials	4,500
Work in Progress	12,000
Finished Goods	14,800
Sales	50,000
Purchases during the year	24,500
Carriage inwards	500
Closing stock-Raw materials	1,500
Work in Progress	4,800
Finished Goods	2,700

3. Calculate the value of opening stock from the following :

	Rs.
Sales	4,00,000
Gross Profit is 25% on cost	
Purchases during the year	2,75,000
Closing stock	15,000

4. Calculate the amount of Profit from the following information :

	Rs.
Capital at the beginning	15,000
Capital at the end	12,500
Drawings during the year	
@ Rs. 400 p.m. for year	4,800

5. From the following Trial Balance of Shri. S. Das prepare a Trading and Profit and Loss Account for the year ended 31st December, 2005 and a Balance Sheet as on that date after making the necessary adjustment:

Dr.	*Rs.*	*Cr.*	*Rs.*
S. Debtors	2,000	S. Creditors	1,400
Drawings	420	Capital	2,500
Stock 1.1.2005	1,200	Sales	7,302
Purchases	6,200	Bank	290
Sales Returns	60	Bad debts	
Wages	900	Provision	210
General Expenses	350		
Fixtures & Equipment	400		
Bad debts	172		
	11,702		11,702

Adjustments :

(i) Closing stock, Rs, 1,470.

(ii) Provide 20% on debtors for Bad debts.

(iii) Included in sales is Rs. 50 being sale of fixtures.

(iv) General Expenses accrued Rs. 25.

(v) Included in Purchases is a new Typewriter, Rs. 1,800 bought on 31st December, 2005

(vi) Depreciate fixtures @ 10% p.a.

6. From the under mentioned Trial Balance of a Trader as on 31st December 2005 prepare a Trading and Profit and Loss Account for the year ended 31st December 2005 and a Balance Sheet as on that date :

Particulars	Dr. *Rs.*	*Particulars*	Cr. *Rs.*
Cash in hand	1,200	Capital a/c	1,00,000
Purchases	1,20,000	Bills Payable	22,000
Stock (opening)	35,000	Sundry Creditors	24,000
Sundry Debtors	50,000	Sales	2,00,200
Plant & Machinery	60,000	Bad debt recovered	1,000
Furniture & Fixture	15,000		
Bills Receivable	20,000		
Rent and Taxes	10,000		
Wages	16,000		
Salaries	20,000		
	3,47,200		3,47,200

Additional information supplied :

(a) Closing Stock Rs. 40,000.

(b) provide outstanding Liabilities, Rent and Taxes Rs. 2,000; Wages Rs. 3,000; Salaries Rs. 4000.

(c) Depreciation : Plant & Machinery 5%; Furniture and Fixture 10%.

(d) Bad Reserve on Sundry Debtors.

7. From the under mentioned Trial Balance of M.R. James as on 31st December 2005 prepare a trading and a profit and loss account for the year ended 31st December 2005 and a Balance Sheet as on that date.

Trial Balance

Particulars	Dr. Rs.	Cr. Rs.
Plant and Machinery	80,000	
Purchases	1,25,000	
Sales		2,30,000
Sundry Creditors		40,000
Stock (Opening)	35,000	
Salaries	16,000	
Sundry Debtors	50,000	
Bad debt Reserve		750
Capital Account		50,000
Bill Receivable	20,000	
Rent and Taxes	5,500	
Furniture and Fixture	2,500	
Bank Loan		20,000
Interest on Loan a/c.	600	
Discount	650	1,200
Bills Payable		9,250
Wages	14,580	
Cash in hand	1,100	
	3,51,200	351,200

The following information is supplied:

(i) Closing stock amounts to Rs. 45,000.

(ii) Outstanding Liabilities to be provided for Rent Rs. 500; Interest Rs. 1,400, and wages Rs. 150.

(iii) Depreciation on Plant and machinery at 5%; Furniture and Fixture at 10%.

(iv) Bad debts Reserve to be raised to on Sundry Debtors.

(v) A Discount Reserve to be made at 1% on Sundry Creditors.

8. From the following Trial Balance of Shri X prepare a Trading and Profit and Loss Account for the year ended 31st December, 2005 and a Balance Sheet as on the date after making necessary adjustments:

Particulars	Dr. Rs.	Particulars	Cr. Rs.
Plant & Machinery	40,000	Capital	60,000
Furniture & Fixtures	12,000	Sales	66,920
Stock (1.1.05)	4,500	Provision for Bad	
Purchase	30,000	& Doubtful Debts	2,500
Sundry Debtors	20,400	Discount	600
Return inward	500	Creditors	9,300
Fire Insurance Premium	900	Bills Payable	5,500
Salary	9,400		
Wages	4,600		
Bills Receivable	8,720		
Bad debts	1,200		
Carriage Outward	600		
Cash at Bank	12,000		
	1,44,820		1,44,820

Adjustments :

(i) Closing Stock Rs. 7,365.

(ii) Sundry Debtors include an item of Rs. 500 for goods supplied to the proprietor and an item of Rs. 550 due from a customer who has become insolvent.

(iii) Depreciate fixed assets @ 10% p.a.

(iv) Goods costing Rs. 1,000 were distributed by way of Advertisement.

(v) The Annual premium of Fire Insurance policy (Rs. 900) was paid for the year commencing on October 1, 2005.

9. From the following Trial Balance prepare necessary Final Accounts :

Particulars	*Rs.*	*Rs.*
Capital & Drawings	3,400	86,140
Purchases & Sales	32,400	88,200
Returns	2,300	2,150
Carriage	1,500	
Lighting & Heating	800	
Water & Gas	3,400	
Wages & Salaries	2,500	
Stock on 1.1.05	7,300	
Rent	900	
Electricity	1,300	
Postage	200	
Printing charges	700	
Law charges	480	
Interest earned		390
Cash in hand	5,600	
Furniture	19,100	
Machinery	60,000	
Buildings	35,000	
	1,76,880	1,76,880

Notes:

Closing stock amounted to Rs. 5,100

Outstanding Expenses wages Rs. 700, Rent 300

Prepaid Printing Charges Rs. 200

Interest earned but not received Rs. 100.

10. The following items appear in the trial balance of a trader on 30th June 2006.

Particulars	*Rs.*	*Particulars*	*Rs.*
Opening Stock	36,000	Miscellaneous Income	566
Sundry Creditors	11,000	Capital a/c	80,000
Sundry debtors	28,000	Commission (Cr.)	2,500
Bills Receivables	16,000	Reserve for doubtful debts	850
Carriage on Purchase	1,200	Purchases	77,000
Wages	13,500	Plant	50,000
Salary	9,900	Sales	1,59,050
Bills payable	6,500	Furniture	9,600
Telephone Expenses	900	Sundry Expenses	900
Repairs	450	Cash at bank and in hand	17,016

Prepare Trading and profit and loss account and the balance sheet after taking the following into consideration.

1. Closing stock Rs. 51,324
2. Unpaid expenses salary Rs. 1600, wages Rs. 2100 and Rent Rs. 4200.
3. Write off 10% on plant, 7½% on furniture as depreciation.
4. Write off Rs. 900 on debtors as bad debts and Increase the balance of the reserve for bad debts by 2½% on debts.
5. The manager is to be paid a commission at 4% on the net profit left after deducting the commission.

11. Mr. Lal started a business on 1st January 2005 with Rs. 10,000 in cash, Rs. 5000 in goods and Rs, 10,000 in furniture. His trial balance as on 31st December 2005 was drawn as follows :

Particulars	Dr. *Rs.*	Cr. *Rs,*
Bad debts	3,500	-
Stock	5,000	-
Furniture	15,000	-
Capital and Drawings	4,500	30,000
Wages	1,800	-
Purchases	18,000	-
Advertisement	1,400	-
Debtors & Creditors	9,000	5,000
Cash	3,200	
Loans secured		2,400
Interest on Loan	400	
Commission	600	
Misc. expenses	700	
Premium	800	
Salaries	2,400	
Reserve for Bad debts		200
Sales		28,700
	66,300	66,300

(i) Goods valued at Rs. 15,000 were destroyed by fire, against this an insurance claim of Rs. 10,000 was to be received. During the year, the proprietor had taken goods of Rs. 2,000 for Personal consumption. The value of the remaining stock in hand was Rs. 8,000.

(ii) Depreciate furniture by 10%. The addition to furniture was made on 1st April.

(iii) Wages include wages of Rs. 800 paid to the workers for repairing furniture.

(iv) Mr. G. debtor for Rs. 2,000 was declared insolvent, only 50 paise in a rupee was receivable against his estate.

(v) Create a Reserve for Bad debts at 5% and Receive for discount at 2% on debtors as well as on creditors.

(vi) Addition to capital was made on 1st July charge interest at 5% on capital and 3% on drawing.

12. The following is the Trial Balance of Subba Rao, a Stationery Merchant as at 31st march 2006 and you are required to prepare a Trading and Profit and Loss Account for the year ended 31st March, 2006 and a Balance Sheet as on that date, after making the necessary adjustment:

Trial Balance

Particulars	*Rs.*	*Rs.*
Capital Account		1,00,000
Drawing Account	12,000	
Plant and Machinery	60,000	
Furniture and Fixture	6,000	
Trade mark Rights (10 years from 1.4.05)	20,000	
Stock on 1.4.97	27,000	
Salaries and Wages	18,200	
Sundry Debtors	22,800	
Sales		1,60,000
Purchases	95,200	
Sundry Creditors		16,800
Rent, Rates and Taxes	6,200	
Trade Expenses	600	
Postage and Telegrams	800	
Bad Debts written off	800	
Loan from G. Gupta (taken from 1st Oct. 2005 at 6% per annum)		10,000
Interest on loan to G. Gupta	200	
Insurance Charges	800	
Sundry Expenses	400	
Cash in hand	1,200	
Cash at Bank	14,600	
	2,86,800	2,86,800

Adjustments : Stock on 31st March, 2006 was valued at Rs. 25,400 of the sundry Debtors Rs. 800 are bad and should be written off; create a Reserve of 5% on Debtors for Doubtful Debts and a Reserve of 2% for Discount on Debtors and a 2% Reserve for Discount on creditors.

Stationery worth Rs. 500 used out of Stock for other than Business purposes.

Goods of the value of Rs. 1,000 were distributed as gifts amongst customers as advertising matter.

Invoices of the value of Rs. 2,400 were recorded in the Sales Books on 27 March, 2006 but the goods were not dispatched until 3rd April, 2006 and were included in the closing Stock.

Depreciate Plant and Machinery by 10%.

Furniture and Fixture by 5 per cent.

13. From the following Trial Balance, draft Trading and Profit and Loss Account for the year ended 31st December, 2005 and a Balance sheet as at that date taking into consideration the following Adjustments :

(1) Closing stock Rs. 9,500.

(2) One quarter of Insurance Premium falls in next year.

(3) Provide 10% depreciation on Furniture.

(4) Loan to X carries 8% interest p.a.

(5) Loan from Y carries 6% interest p.a.

(6) Goods worth Rs, 500 have been taken up by the proprietor for private use.

(7) Provide 5% for bad and doubtful debts.

(8) Salaries include salary to proprietor @ Rs. 200 p.m.

Debit Balance	*Rs.*	*Credit Balance*	*Rs.*
Stock 1.1.2005	6,000	Capital	40,000
Salaries	6,000	Return outwards	500
Drawings	6,000	Loan from Y	5,000
Carriage Inwards	1,000	Rent outstanding	100
Carriage outwards	500	Creditors	13,000
Returns Inwards	800	Liabilities for other expenses	1,900
Loan to X	3,000	Provision for	
Rent	1,200	Bad Debts	1,000
Purchases	60,000	Discount	300
Debtors	30,000	Sales	73,700
Advertisement	3,000	Rent by subletting	500
Bad Debts	500		
Discount	600		
Cash	200		
Furniture	3,000		
Goodwill	15,000		
Wages	100		
Insurance Premium	600		
Bank	8,500		
	1,36,000		1,36,000

14. From the following trial Balance as on 31st March 2006. Prepare trading and profit and loss account for the year ended 31st March, 2006 and a Balance sheet as on that date:

Particulars	Dr. *Rs.*	Cr. *Rs.*
Plant & Machinery	20,000	
Building	20,000	
Furniture and Fixtures	14,000	
Sundry Debtors	1,06,300	
Cash in hand	3,000	
Cash at Bank	52,000	
Travelling Expenses	5,000	
Bad debts	900	
Goods returned	8,000	4,000
Purchases	72,000	
Sales		1,28,000
Wages	18,000	
Salaries	18,000	
Office Rent	3,600	
Insurance	2,000	
Commission	1,200	
Interest on Loan	6,000	
Office General Exp.	2,400	
Publicity Exps.	6,000	
Sundry Creditors		12,000
Loan		50,000
Opening Stock	56,000	
Capital		2,64,400
Drawings	44,000	
	4,58,400	4,58,400

Additional information :

(i) Closing Stock was valued at Rs. 88,000.

(ii) Rent paid during the year was for 10 months.

(iii) Wages outstanding were Rs. 6,000.

(iv) Bad debts to be written off during the year were Rs. 1,200. A provision for bad debt is to be created @ 5% on Debtors.

(v) Depreciation to be provided as follows:- Plant & Machinery @ 10%. Building @ and furniture and fixture @ 10%.

(vi) A commission of 1% of the Net Profit after charging such commission is to be allowed to the Manager.

15. In a trial balance, debtors appear at Rs. 12,000 and creditors at Rs. 7,000. Make provision for bad and doubtful debts at 5% on debtors and provisions for discount on debtors and creditors at 2.5%, after considering the fact that included in the debtors is the amount of Rs. 2,000 due from X and included in creditors is the amount of Rs. 1,000 due to him.

Give journal entries for making provisions.

16. Following is the trial balance of Mr. Mahesh as on 31.12.05.

Particulars	Dr. *Rs.*	Cr. *Rs.*
Purchases and sales	1,80,000	2,05,000
Opening stock	10,000	-
Salaries less P.F.	5,400	-
P.F. remittance including		
Proprietor's contribution 50%	1,200	-
Rent @ Rs. 250 p.m.	2,750	-
Machinery	29,000	-
Wages	3,000	-
Furniture & Fitting's	5,000	-
Electricity	550	-
Trade Expenses	1,500	-
Debtors & creditors	10,500	15,000
Interest on Loan	900	-
Commission	200	-
Buildings	30,000	-
Loan (Int. @ 10%)	-	10,000
Capital	-	55,000
Drawings	5,000	
	2,85,000	2,85,000

Prepare Trading and Profit and loss account for the year 2005 and the Balance sheet as at 31.1.2005 taking the following information :

(i) On 1.1.05 machinery worth Rs. 5,000 was sold for Rs. 9,000 and credited to Machinery account.

(ii) Wages include Rs. 1,000 paid for machinery erection charges.

(iii) Purchases include cost of Moped scooter for Rs. 5,000.

(iv) The proprietor has taken goods costing Rs. 1,000 for which no entry has been made.

(v) Sundry debtors include Rs. 500 which have become bad.

(vi) Provide 10% reserve for bad debts.

(vii) Electricity outstanding is Rs. 50.

(viii) Goods costing Rs. 5,000 was destroyed by fire and insurance claim was received for Rs. 4,000.

(ix) Provide depreciation at 10% on machinery, furniture and Moped and 5% on Buildings.

(x) Value of closing stock Rs. 12,000.

17. From the following balances extracted from the books of Sri Ramananda prepare the Trading and profit & Loss Account for the year ended 30th Nov. 2005 and the Balance sheet as on that date:

Particulars	*Rs.*
Plant & Machinery	7,00,000
Land & Buildings	1,15,000
Purchases	5,00,000
Stock (1.12.04)	2,00,000
Sales	12,34,000
Office salaries & Expenses	70,000
Advertisement	21,500
Carriage Inwards	10,000
Sundry Creditors	4,71,000
Loan (Cr.)	40,000
Carriage outwards	6,000
Wages	2,00,000
Bad debts provision	10,000
Capital	6,10,000
Office rent and Insurance	42,000
Printing and stationery	10,000
Works manager's Salary	56,000
Factory expenses	59,000
Cash in hand	500
Cash at Bank	52,000
Sundry Debtors	2,62,000
Drawings	61,000

The following further information is given :

1. Stock on 30th Nov. 2005 is valued at Rs. 2,10.000 included in the stock are goods valued at Rs. 10,000 which are sold out but not yet delivered too the purchaser.
2. Depreciate plant and Machinery at 10% and land and buildings 2½%.
3. Interest on loan at 6% per annum is in arrears.
4. Bad debts of Rs. 5000 are to be written off on Sundry debtors.
5. Bad debts provision is to be kept at 5% on debtors.
6. Purchases account includes goods of the value of Rs. 1000 used by the proprietor for his personal and private purpose.

18. R.K. Menon is a general manager and he keeps his books in double entry system. This financial year ends on 31st March 2006.

The following are ledger balances

	Particulars	*Rs.*	*Rs.*
1.	Capital	-	1,00,000
2.	Heritable property at cost	50,000	-
3.	Plant and Machinery	40,000	-
4.	Motor lorries	10,000	-
5.	Investments	5,000	-
6.	Stock on 31.3.05	3,00,000	-
7.	Purchases	8,00,000	-
8.	Sales	-	12,00,000
9.	Carriage Inward	10,000	-
10.	Wages and Salaries	1,50,000	-

Contd...

11.	Rates and Insurance	500	-
12.	Repairs to buildings and plants	1,500	-
13.	Alternation of plant and buildings	4,500	-
14.	Motor lorry expenses	8,500	-
15.	Legal Expenses	400	-
16.	Bank Interest	2000	-
17.	Interest and Investment less tax	-	300
18.	Interest on advance	-	200
19.	Payment of income tax		
20.	Income tax advance payment	8,000	
21.	Purchase Ledger Balance		4,70,000
22.	Sales Ledger Balance	5,00,000	
23.	Bad Debt Reserve		20,000
24.	Income Tax	50,000	
25.	Bank Overdraft		2,00,000
26.	Bills Receivable	50,000	
27.	Cash in hand	100	
		19,90,500	19,90,500

The stock as at 31.3.2006 was taken at cost at Rs. 5,50,000 and the following adjustment are required to be made:

Wages unpaid Rs. 2,000, Rates accrued Rs. 200, General Expenses unpaid Rs. 500, Bank interest accrued Rs. 200, Insurance prepaid Rs. 50, Motor Licence unexpired Rs. 70 Write off cost of Alternation to Plant and Building : Charge depreciation on the value of the following assets. Heritable property $1\frac{1}{4}$ percent, plant and Machinery $7\frac{1}{2}\%$, Motor Lorries $33\frac{1}{3}$ per cent.

Prepare Trading and Profit and Loss Account for the year ending 31.3.2006 the balance sheet as at that date.

19. Following was the Trial Balance of Mr. Bharat at 31st December, 2006 prepare final accounts.

Particulars	Dr. *Rs.*	Cr. *Rs.*
Capital	-	4,000
Plant and Machinery	5,000	-
Furniture & Fittings	260	-
Stock as on 1st Jan. 2004	4,800	-
Motor Vans	1,200	-
Sundry debtors & creditors	4,570	5,200
Cash in hand	40	-
Cash at Bank	650	-
Wages	15,000	-
Salaries	1,400	-
Purchases & sales	21,350	48,000
Bills Receivable & Bills Payable	720	560
Returns	930	550
Provision for Doubtful debts	-	250
Drawings	700	-
Rent	600	-
Factory lighting and heating	80	-
Insurance	630	-
General expenses	100	-
Bad debts	250	-
Discount	650	370
	58,930	58,930

The following adjustments are to be made:

(i) Stock on 31st December 2005 Rs. 5,200.

(ii) 3 Months factory lighting and heating charges, but not paid Rs. 30.

(iii) 5% depreciation to be written off on furniture.

(iv) Write off further bad debts Rs. 70.

(v) The provision for doubtful debts to be increased to Rs. 300 and provision for discount on debtors @ 2% to be made.

(vi) During the year machinery was purchased for Rs. 2000, but it was debited to purchases account.

20. From the following trial balance of Mr. G. Singh for the year ending 31.3.2005 and additional information given, prepare trading and profit and loss account and balance sheet as on that date.

Trial Balance

Particulars	Dr. Rs.	Cr. Rs.
Opening Stock	62,500	-
Capital	-	4,64,000
Debtors and Creditors	75,000	43,750
Purchases and Sales	5,00,000	8,75,000
Carriage	10,000	-
Wages and Salaries	31,250	
Commission	-	16,750
Machinery	1,38,750	-
Furniture	25,000	-
Bad debts received	-	8,000
B/R and B/P	37,500	33,750
Land and Buildings	5,00,000	-
Taxes and Insurance	21,250	-
10% Bank Loan	-	50,000
Interest on Bank loan	3,000	-
Bank	24,500	
Drawings	62,500	
	14,91,250	14,91,250

Additional Information :

(i) Value of the closing stock as on 31st March 2006 is Rs. 50,000.

(ii) Wages and salaries outstanding Rs. 12,500 and Insurance prepaid is Rs. 5000.

(iii) Depreciate machinery and furniture @ 10% and 15% per annum respectively. Machinery included a machine which was purchased for Rs. 38,500 on 30th Sept. 2005.

(iv) Goods costing Rs. 10,000 uses taken by the proprietor for his personal use, but no entry has been made in the books of accounts.

[Delhi B.Com (Pass) 2002(B)]

21. You are required to prepare trading and profit and loss account and balance sheet from the following balances and adjustments for the year ending on 31.12.2005.

Particulars	Dr. Rs.	Cr. Rs.
Purchases/Sales	1,30,295	1,80,500
Cash in hand	500	-
Cash at Bank	9,500	-
Stock on 1.1.2004	40,000	-
Wags	22,525	-
Returns	2,400	195
Repairs	1,675	-
Debtors/creditors	30,000	30,305
Bad debts	2,310	-
Loan (12% p.a.)	-	20,000
Discounts	800	530
Capital	-	37,500
Interest on loan	600	-
Salaries	8,000	-
Sales tax	800	-
Octroi	500	-
Insurance	1,000	-
Charity	125	-
Rent	2,000	-
Machinery	16,000	-
	2,69,030	2,69,030

Adjustments :

(i) Wages include Rs. 2000 for erection of new machine installed on 1.1.2005.

(ii) Provide for depreciation on Machinery @ 5% p.a.

(iii) Closing stock is Rs. 40,925.

(iv) Salaries unpaid Rs. 800

(v) Further bad debts Rs. 400

(vi) Make a provision of 5% on debtors for doubtful debts.

(vii) Rent is paid up to 31st March, 2006.

(viii) Unexpired in insurance Rs. 300.

[Delhi B. Com (Pass) 2004]

22. Following is the trial balance of Mr. Ram for the year ending on 30th June 2006.

Particulars	Dr. Rs.	Cr. Rs.
Capital		20,500
Creditors		15,000
Outstanding expenses		3,500
Rent received		300
Purchases Return		2,000
Sales		1,44,800
Reserve for Bad debts		300
Advertisement Development	4,000	
Plant and Machinery	10,000	
Goodwill	2,500	
Agents Samples	1,350	

Contd...

Cash in hand	55	
Drawings	2,600	
Purchases	85,500	
Carriage Inwards	750	
Wages	11,500	
Power	4,000	
Depreciation of Machinery	500	
Salary	17,200	
Dividend Received		900
General Expenses	4,100	
Prepaid expenses	200	
Salary of agent	4,550	
Rent and Insurance	9,950	
Discount allowed	2,500	
Sales returns	300	
Commission to Agent	1,445	
Stock	16,000	
Debtors	7,300	
Cash in bank	1,000	
	1,87,300	1,87,300

Adjustments :

(1) Closing stock was valued at Rs. 15,700. Goods costing Rs. 1,000 was destroyed by fire. The Insurance company admitted the claim for Rs. 800 only.

(2) Write off Rs. 500 as bad debts and create a reserve for doubtful debts on debtors @5%.

(3) Depreciate Agent samples by $33\frac{1}{3}\%$.

(4) Write off advertisement development by 25%.

(5) Charge 5% Manager's Commission after charging his commission.

(6) The Proprietor withdrew Rs. 100 for his private use. This amount was included in general expenses. You are required to prepare trading and profit and loss for the your ended 30th June 2006 and the balance sheet as on that date.

23. From the following Trial balance of a trader on March 31,2006, prepare Trading and Profit and Loss account for the year ending 31st March 2006 and Balance sheet as at that date after giving effect to the under mentioned adjustments:

Debit balances	*Rs.*	*Credit balances*	*Rs.*
Drawing balances	6,000	Bank Overdraft	25,000
Wages	15,500	Interest on Investment	5,800
Stock	12,800	Bills Payable	4,600
Loan to X	4,000	Interest on want to X	320
Rent	5,000	Capital	1,00,000
General Expenses	1,480	Reserve for bad and doubtful debts	250
Investments	60,000	Sales	2,30,000
Purchases	1,60,000	Sundary Creditors	12,590
Freight and carriage	2,100		
Goodwill	40,000		
Bills Reviewable	6,200		

Contd...

Rates and Taxes	1,800		
Sales Returns	2,100		
Insurance	900		
Cash and bank balances	3,700		
Postage and telegram	3,800		
Land and buildings	25,000		
Plant and machinery	10,000		
Sundry debtors	16,500		
Packing charges	400		
Bad debtors	1,280		
	3,78,560		3,78,560

Adjustments-

(i) Closing stock as at 31.3.2006 Rs. 16,000

(ii) Goods worth Rs. 700 were sent on 25.3.2006 as sale on approval basis for Rs. 800 and the approval was not received before the end of the month.

(iii) 20% of the goodwill is to be written off

(iv) Further bad debts were estimated at Rs. 350. Increase reserve for bad debts to the extent of Rs. 1500.

(v) Depreciate land and building by 3% and plant & machinery by 10%

(vi) Goods worth Rs. 800 were distributed as free samples

[Delhi, B Com. (Pass) 2006]

ANSWERS

B. Objective Type Questions

(a) (I)

(b) (III)

(c) (II)

(d) (III)

(a) F (b) T (c) F (d) T (e) F.

C. Exercises

	Rs.
1.	20,000
2.	28,000
3.	60,000
4.	2,300
5. (i) Gross Profit	2,162
(ii) Net Profit	1,385
(iii) Total of Balance Sheet	5,180
6. (i) Gross Profit	66,200
(ii) Net Profit	25,450
(iii) Total of Balance Sheet	1,80,450

7. Gross Profit	1,00,000
(ii) Net Profit	72,200
(iii) Total of balance sheet	1,93,100
8. Gross profit	35,685
(ii) Net Profit	18,110
(iii) total of Balance sheet	92,410
9. (i) Gross Profit	45,550
(ii) Net Profit	41,360
(iii) Total of balance sheet	1,25,100
10.(i) Gross Profit	80,574
(ii) Net Profit	56,567
(iii) Total of Balance sheet	1,64,280
11. (i) Gross Profit	29,700
(ii) Net Profit	10,352
(iii) Total of Balance Sheet	42,017
12. (i) Gross Profit	62,000
(ii) Net Profit	22,418
(iii) Total of balance sheet	1,36,982
13. (i) Gross Profit	16,300
(ii) Net Profit	6,390
(iii) Total of Balance Sheet	57,790
14. (i) Gross Profit	60,000
(ii) Net Profit	3,787
(iii) Total of balance sheet	2,92,945
15. (i) Amount of provision for bad and doubtful debts	500
(ii) Provision for discount on debtors	23,750
(iii) Provision for discount on creditors	15,000
16. (i) Gross profit	36,000
(ii) Net Profit	14,200
(iii) Total of Balance sheet	88,600
17. (i) Gross profit	4,10,000
(ii) Net profit	1,77,375
(iii) Total of balance sheet	12,38,775
18. (i) Gross profit	4,88,000
(ii) Net Profit	4,63,362
(iii) Total of balance	11,86,262
19. (i) Gross profit	13,560
(ii) Net profit	10,083
(iii) Total of balance sheet	19,173
20. (i) Gross profit	3,18,750
(ii) Net Profit	3,06,550

(iii) Total of Balance sheet	8,40,050
21. (i) Gross profit	27,900
(ii) Net profit	6,440
(iii) Total of balance sheet	96,845
22. (i) Gross Profit	45,450
(ii) Net Profit	4,110
(iii) Total of balance sheet	40,615
23. (i) Gross Profit	54,200
(ii) Net Profit	33,510
(iii) Total of balance sheet	1,69,700

CHAPTER 12

ACCOUNTING CONCEPT OF INCOME

A. Essay Type Questions

1. What may be the possible reasons for an increase in the size of gross profit of current year as compared to previous year?

   [Delhi, B.Com. (Pass), 1973, 80, 83, 89; Delhi, B.Com. (Hons.) 1985]

2. (a) What is income? State the factors that influence the measurement of income.

   [Delhi, B.Com. (Pass), 2001]

   (b) Do you agree with the following statements? Give reasons:

   (i) Gross profit is increased only due to decrease in price of goods purchased?

   [Delhi, B. Com. (Pass), 1990 (supple.)]

   (ii) "Change in selling price is the only reason which is responsible for change in gross profit."

   [Delhi, B. Com. (Pass), 1991]

   (iii) "Change in net profits are mostly affected by changes in gross profits."

   [Delhi, B. Com. (Pass), 1991(B)]

B. Objective Types Questions

1. State whether each of the following statement is true or false.

   (a) Revenue is recognized only when goods are sold.

   (b) Business income also includes the personal income of the owner of the business.

   (c) Change in revenue is because of changes in quantity and sale price both.

2. Fill in the blanks:-

   (i) The revenue is generally recognized when goods/services are__________

   (ii) The business income includes _________net income.

   (iii) Change in revenue is because of changes in _________ and _______both.

C. Exercises

1. Explain the accounting concept of income and analyse the increase in gross profit from the following data:

	Dec. 31, 2005	Dec. 31, 2006
	Rs.	Rs.
Sales	4,800	8,400
Cost of sales	4,000	6,400
Quantity sold	80 metres	100 metres

2. The following is a comparative statement of Company X :

	2006	2005
	Rs.	Rs.
Net sales	2,53,000	2,00,000
Cost of goods sold	1,81,125	1,50,000
Gross profit	71,875	50,000

The following is the additional information :

	2006	2005
	Rs.	Rs.
Units sold	1,150	1,000
Selling price per unit	220	200
Unit cost	157.50	150.00

Prepare a statement showing the effect of different causes that are responsible for a change in gross profit.

3. Find out the % changes in :
   (a) Volume, and
   (b) Selling price,

The data given are :

	2005	2006
Sales	10,000	14,000
Cost of goods sold	8,000	10,000
Gross profit	2,000	4,000

The cost increased in 2006 by 8% than 2005

4. Assume the following data :

2006	2005	
Sales	13,35,180	11,00,000
Cost of goods sold	11,67,790	9,00,000
Gross profit on sales	1,67,390	2,00,000

If costs increased by 9 per cent in 2006 what were the percentage changes in?
   (a) Volume and
   (b) Selling price,

5. Following are comparative statements of a wholesale distributing company for the years 2005 and 2006

	2005	2006	Change
	Rs.	Rs.	Rs
Sales revenue	1,00,000	1,15,500	+15,500
Cost of sales	60,000	75,600	+ 15,600
Gross profit	-40,000	39,000	-100

Prepare statements analysis showing the change in gross profit under the following independent assumption :

Volume of sales was 10% higher during 2006.

ANSWERS

B. Objective types Questions

1. (a) T (b) F (c) T
2. (i) Sold/rendered
   (ii) Realized
   (iii) Quantity and price

C. Exercises

1. Revenue increase of Rs. 3,600 is caused because of (i) increase in quantity sold Rs. 1,200, (ii) increase in sale price Rs. 1920 and increase in both Rs. 480, while increase in cost of Rs. 400 is because of increase in quantity sold Rs. 1000, Cost Rs. 1,120 and both Rs. 280.
2. Increase in sales (revenue) is caused because of

(i)	Increase in selling price	Rs. 53,000
	Due to	Rs.
	(a) Increase in Quantity	= 30,000
	150 x 200	
	(b) Increase in Price	= 20,000
	20 x 1000	
	(c) both (quantity Price)	= 3,000
	150 x 20	= 53,000
(ii)	Increase in cost of sales	= 31,125
	(a) Increase in Qty	= 22,500
	150 x 150	
	(b) Increase in price	= 7,500
	7.50 x 1000	
	(c) both 7.50 x 150	= 1,125
		= 31,125

3 (i) Change in volume = 15.74%
  (ii) Change in selling price = 20.96%
4. (i) increase in volume = 19%
   (ii) % increase in selling price = 2%
5. When volume increases by 10%
   (i) % increase in volume = 5%
   (ii) % change in price = 14.54%

CHAPTER 13

ACCOUNTS OF NON-TRADING ORGANIZATIONS

A. Essay Type Questions

1. What is an Income and expenditure account how it is prepared and by whom?
2. Distinguish between -
   (i) Income and expenditure account and receipts and payments account.
   [Delhi B. Com (Pass) 2003, 2005, 2006(B)]
   [Delhi B. Com (Hons) 2003]
   (ii) Capital receipts and revenue receipts.
   [Delhi, B. Com. (Pass) 2004, 2005]
   (iii) Capital expenditure and revenue expenditure.
   [Delhi B. Com (Pass) 2005]
3. How will you deal with (i) specific donation and (ii) legacy in the final account of a non-trading concern?
   [Delhi B. Com. (Pass) 1999, Delhi, B. Com (Hons) 1999]

B. Objective Type Questions

1. Do you agree with the following statement
   (i) The closing balance of receipt and payment accounts reveals surplus or deficit of a non-trading concern.
   (ii) The closing balance of income and expenditure account reveals cash in hand or over draft of a non trading concern.
2. Indicate the correct answers in the following
   I. Receipts and Payments a/c is
      (i) Nominal a/c
      (ii) Real a/c
      (iii) Personal a/c
      (iv) None of the above
   II. Income and expenditure a/c is
      (i) Real a/c
      (ii) Personal a/c
      (iii) Nominal a/c
      (iv) None of the above
   III. Non Profit organization prepare
      (i) Profit and loss a/c
      (ii) Income and expenditure a/c
      (iii) Trading and profit and loss a/c
      (iv) None of the above

C. Exercises

1. Calculate the amount of salaries to be shown in Receipts and Payment Account.

		Rs.
(i)	Salaries as per income and expenditure account	1,500
(ii)	Salaries paid in advance in previous year	700
(iii)	Salary outstanding at the end of current year	300
(iv)	Salary outstanding at the end of previous year	800

[Delhi. B. Com. (Pass) 1990]

2. How will you deal with the following case, while preparing the final accounts as on Dec. 31,05

Balance Sheet
(as on 1st Jan. 2005)

Liabilities	Rs.	Assets	Rs.
Creditors for stationery	225	Stationery	300

Receipts and payments account
For the year ended 31st Dec., 2005

Receipts	Rs.	Payments	Rs.
To Sale of stationery	125	(Purchase of stationery)	5,000

Additional Information

	Rs.
Stationery on 31st December, 2005	800

3. How will you deal with the following in the Income and Expenditure Account and the Balance Sheet of a club as on 31st December, 2005.

Receipts		Rs.	Payments	Rs.
To Subscriptions				
	Rs.			
2004	450			
2005	4,800			
2006	600	5,850		

Additional Information :

		Rs.
(i)	Subscriptions outstanding as on 31st Dec. 04	750
(ii)	Subscription outstanding as on 31st Dec. 05	1,250
(iii)	Subscriptions received in advance as on 31st Dec. 04	600

4. Calculate the amount of 'stationery sued' to be shown in Income and Expenditure Account from the following data :

(i) Amount paid for stationery as per Receipts and Payments Account Rs. 4000.

(ii) Stationery bill outstanding Rs. 1,000 in the beginning and Rs. 200 at the end of the year.

(iii) Stationery in hand at the beginning Rs. 2,000 and at the end Rs. 1,500.

[Delhi, B. Com. (Pass), 1990 (supple.)]

5. Calculate the amount of donations to be shown in Income and Expenditure Account and outstanding at the end of 2006 from the data of Nav Jagriti Kala Sangam.

   (i) Donations received during 2006 - Rs. 2,900

   (ii) Donations outstanding in 2005 was Rs. 800

   (iii) Donations received in 2006 includes Rs. 700 for 2005 and Rs. 600 for 2007.

   (iv) Donations received in advance for 2006 in 2005 was Rs. 400.

   (v) There are 150 members each paying annual donation of Rs. 25.

[Delhi, B. Com. (Pass), 1991 (B)]

6. Calculate amount of salaries to be shown in Receipt and Payment Account

1.	Salaries as per Income & Expenditure a/c	Rs. 2,500
2.	Paid in advance in previous year	Rs. 700
3.	Outstanding at the end of current year	Rs. 1,300
4.	Outstanding at the end of previous year	Rs. 1,800

7. How will you deal with the following information in the Income and Expenditure account for the year ended 31st March, 2006 and Balance Sheet of a Club as on 31st March, 2006

	Rs.
Subscriptions received during the year ended March 31, 2006	45,000
Subscriptions in arrears on 31st March, 2005	5,000
Subscriptions in arrears on 31st March, 2006	8,000
Subscriptions received in advance as on 31st March 2005	6,000
Subscriptions received in advance as on 31st March, 2006	1,500

[Delhi, B. Com. (Hons.) 1yr. 1991 (supplementary)]

8. The following the summary of cash transactions of a Literary Club for the year ended 31st December, 2006

Particulars	Rs.	Particulars	Rs.
Balance from Last Year	319	Rent and Rates	198
Entrance Fees	255	Wages	215
Subscriptions	1,600	Lighting Charges	87
Donations	165	Lecturer's Fees	400
Life Membership Fees	250	Books	213
Interest	12	Office Expenses	470
Profit on Entertainments	44	Placed on 6% Fixed Deposit 1st July, 2006	800
		Cash in hand	62
		Cash at Bank	200
	2,645		2,645

At the beginning of the year, the club possessed books worth Rs. 2,000 and furniture Rs. 850. Ordinary subscriptions in arrears at the beginning of the year amount to Rs. 35 and at the end of the year Rs. 45 and six months rent (Rs. 60) was due at the beginning of the year and at the end of the year.

Prepare Income and Expenditure Account of the Club for the year ended 31st December, 2006 and its Balance Sheet on that date after providing for depreciation Rs. 113 and Rs. 50 on books and furniture respectively.

9. The following is the Receipts and Payments Account of a Cultural Society for the year ending December, 2006.

Receipts and Payments Account
(for the year ended 31st December, 2006)

Receipts		Rs.	Payments	Rs.
To Cash in hand 2006		1,500	By Bank Overdraft on 1st Jan., 2006	3,100
To Subscriptions			By Investment in Securities	3,000
2005	200		By Furniture	1,450
2006	16,200		By Salary	6,200
2007	250	16,650	By Printing and Stationery	890
To Proceeds from Entertainment		2,000	By Cost of Entertainments	1,710
To Entrance Fees		670	By Sundry Expenses	1,420
Interest on Securities		480	By Balance on 31.12.2006:	
To Sale of old chairs (book value nil)		120	Cash	550
			Bank	3,100
		21,420		21,420

You are required to prepare the Income and Expenditure Account of the Cultural Society in respect of the year ended 31st December, 2006 and a balance sheet as at that date having due regard to the following:

(i) The society has 1,800 members each paying annual subscriptions of Rs. 10, subscriptions amounting Rs. 90 were in arrears in respect of the year 2005

(ii) Stock of stationery at 31st December, 2005 was Rs. 125 and 31st December, 2006 Rs. 87.

(iii) Entrance fees are to be capitalized.

(iv) Salary of Rs. 550 for December, 2006 is outstanding. Expenses accrued at 31st December, 2005 amounted to Rs. 132. The society has paid Rs. 500 in the year 2005 in the year 2005 towards telephone charges of which Rs. 125 pertained to the year 2006.

(v) At 31st December 2005 Premises stood in the books at Rs. 24,500 and Investment at Rs. 6,500. Depreciate premises and furniture by 5%.

[Delhi, B. Com. (Pass) 1998 (modified)]

10. Given below is the Receipts and Payments Account of a Club for the year ending 31st December, 2006:

Receipts and Payments Account, 1996

Receipts	Rs.	Payments	Rs.
To Balance	1,025	By Salaries	600
To Subscriptions:		By Expenses	75
2005	40	By Drama Expenses	450
2006	2,050	By Newspapers	150
2007	60	By Municipal Taxes	40
To Donations	540	By Charity	350
To Sale of Drama Tickets	950	By Investments	2,000
To Sale of Waste Paper	45	By Electric Charges	145
		By Balance	900
	4,710		4,710

Prepare the Club's Income and Expenditure Account for the year ended 31st December and its Balance Sheet as at that date after taking the following information into account.

(1) There are 500 members each paying an annual subscription of Rs. 5, Rs. 50 being in arrears for 2005.

(2) Municipal taxes amounting to Rs. 40 per annum have been paid up to March 31, 2007 and Rs. 50 for salaries is outstanding.

(3) Building stands in the books at Rs. 5,000.

(4) 6% interest has accrued on investments for five months.

[Delhi, B. Com. (Pass), 1991]

11. The following is the Receipts and Payments Account 2006 and Balance Sheet for the year 2005. Prepare Income and Expenditure Account and Balance Sheet for the year 2006.

Receipts and Payments Account for 2006

Receipts	Rs.	Payments	Rs.
To Balance 1.1.06	10,000	By Expenses 2005	1,200
To Subscriptions:		2006	2,000
2005	200	By Land	4,000
2006	2,100	By Interest	400
2007	100	By Miscellaneous Expenses	2000
To Entrance Fees	800	By Balance 31.12.2006	8,300
To Lockers Rent	700		
To Miscellaneous Incomes	4,000		
	17,900		17,900

Balance Sheet
(as on 31st December, 2005)

Liabilities	Rs.	Assets	Rs.
Capital Fund	33,620	Buildings	30,000
Subscriptions Received in Advance	600	Outstanding Subscriptions	380
Outstanding Expenses	1,400	Outstanding Lockers Rent	240
Loan	5,000	Cash	10,000
	40,620		40,620

12. The following is the Receipts and Payments a/c of an Amusement Club :

Receipts and Payments Account
(for the year ended 31st December, 2006)

Receipts		Rs.	Payments	Rs.
To Balance b/d :			By Salary of Secretary	3,600
Cash	60		By Honorarium	450
Bank	3,000	3,060	By Wages	2,400
To Subscriptions (Including subscriptions			By Charities	2,000
for 1997 Rs. 150)		9,000	By Printing & Stationery	300
To Sale of Furniture on Jan. 1, 06		750	By Postage	100
To Sale of Newspapers		50	By Rent and Taxes	1,200
To Legacies		3,000	By Upkeep of the Land	500
To Interest on Investment			By Sports Materials	2,500

Contd...

(Cost of investments Rs. 20,000)	1,200	By Balance c/d	14,850
To Endowment Find Receipts	10,000		
To Proceeds of Concerts	800		
To Advertisement in the Year Book	40		
	27,900		27,900

Current assets and liabilities on December 31, 2005 and 2006 were as follows :

	31.12.2005	On 31.12.2006
Subscriptions in arrears	200	450
Subscriptions in advance	300	600
Furniture	2,000	1,080

Depreciation was @ 10% p.a. on the furniture left after selling a part of it.

It was decided that half of the legacies may be capitalized.

Prepare Income and Expenditure a/c and the Balance Sheet as on that date.

13. From the following Trial Balance of a School, prepare Income and Expenditure Account for the year ending 31st March,, 2006 and Balance Sheet as on that date :

Trial Balance

Debit Balances	Amount Rs.	Credit Balances	Amount Rs.
Land	50,000	Capital Fund	15,60,000
Buildings	15,00,000	Tuition fees received	25,10,000
Furniture	3,00,000	Salaries Payable	1,75,000
Salaries-Teaching Staff	12,00,000	Prize Fund	2,00,000
Admn. Staff	2,60,000	Tournament Found	3,00,000
Investments	7,00,000	General Reserve Fund	2,00,000
Postage and Stationery	1,73,0000	Interest received	
Lighting	36,000	on investments	77,000
General Expenses	65,000	Donations for the Hall	1,50,000
Prizes Awarded	20,000		
Tournament Expenses	30,000		
Library Books	3,75,000		
Bank Balance	4,63,000		
	51,72,000		51,72,000

Adjustments

1. Depreciate Buildings 20%; Furniture 10% and Library Books by 20%.
2. The investments were made against the various funds commonly.

[Delhi B. Com. (Pass) 1997 (modified)]

14. From the following Receipts and Payments Account of Mumbai Club, prepare Income and Expenditure Account for the year ending 31st December, 2005 and a Balance Sheet as on that date:

Receipts and Payments Accounts

Receipts	Amount Rs.	Payments	Amount Rs.
Cash in Hand (opening)	4,000	Salary	2,000
Cash at Bank (opening)	10,000	Repairs Expenses	500
Donations	5,000	Purchase of Furniture	6,000
Subscriptions	12,000	Miscellaneous Expenses	500
Entrance fees	1,000	Purchase of Investments	6,000
Interest on Investments	100	Insurance Premium	200
Interest Received from bank	400	Billiards Table	8,000
Sale of old Newspapers	150	Paper, Ink, etc.	150
Sale of Drama Tickets	1,050	Drama Expenses	500
		Cash in Hand (Closing)	2,650
		Cash at Bank (Closing)	7,200
	33,700		33,700

Additional Information

1. Subscriptions in arrears for 2005 are Rs. 900 and subscriptions received in advance for the year 2006 are Rs. 350.
2. Insurance Premium outstanding Rs. 40.
3. Misc. Expenses prepaid Rs. 90.
4. Entrance fees are to be treated as revenue income.
5. Interest on Investments has accrued @ 8% for 5 months.
6. Billiards Table costing Rs. 30,000 was purchased last year and Rs. 22,000 was paid for it.
7. Donations are to be capitalized to the extent of 50%.

[CA Foundation, Nov. 1997 (modified)]

15. From the following Trial Balance, Prepare a on Income and Expenditure account of Delhi club for the year ended:

31st December, 2006 and a Balance Sheet as on that date. Depreciate Furniture by 10%, Billiards Table and Accessories by 20% and China, Glass, Cutlery etc. by $33\frac{1}{3}\%$ of the subscriptions, Rs. 400 is paid in advance and Rs. 250 is in arrears. Rs. 300 is owing for salaries to staff.

Dr. Balances	Rs.
Furniture	2,500
Billiards Table & Accessories (bought in 2004)	1,250
China, Glass, Cutlery etc.	333
Repairs	734
Salaries & Wages	2,262
Rent and Telephone	3,194
Fuel and Light	1,618
Cost of Entertainments	2,190
Sundry Expenses	1,600
Cost of Annual Dinner	760
Sundry Debtors	1,170
Cash at Bank	4,800

Cash in hand	174
Cr. Balances	22,585
Members Subscriptions	10,560
Sale of Tickets for Entertainment	3,234
Sundry Creditors	2,600
Entrance Fees	448
Income and Expenditure a/c Balance	4,000
Sundry Receipts from Billiards etc.	1,743
	22,585

[Delhi, B. Com. (Pass), 1999]

16. The following is the Receipts and Payments Account of Mehrauli Club for the year ended 31st December, 2006

Receipts		Rs.	Payments	Rs.
To Cash in hand (1.1.06)		350	By Bank Overdraft (1.1.06)	180
To Subscriptions:			By Salaries	670
2005	400		By Printing & Stationery	50
2006	2,200		By Furniture	1,000
2007	100	2,700	By Investment Securities	1,500
To Income from Entertainment		230	By Balance as on 31.12.2006	
To Entrance Fee		450	Cash in hand	170
To Interest on Securities		560	Cash at Bank	900
To Sale of Old Furniture (Book value 150)		180		
		4,470		4,470

Prepare Income and Expenditure Account for the year ended 31st December, 2006 and the Balance Sheet as on that date having due regard to the following additional information :

(i) The club has 250 members paying an annual subscription of Rs. 10 each.

(ii) Salary Rs. 50 was outstanding on 1.1.06 and Rs. 60 is still payable for the year 2006.

(iii) The club had furniture Rs. 2,650, Building Rs. 5,000 and Investments Rs. 7,000 as on 1.1.06

(iv) Depreciate Building and Furniture by 5% of their closing balance.

17. The Calcutta Association submits to you its Receipts and Payments Account for the year ending 31st December, 2006. You are required to prepare the Income and Expenditure Account and the Balance Sheet relating to the year:

Receipts	Rs.	Payments	Rs.
To Opening Balance :		By Establishment	
Cash in hand	250	(Including Rs. 400 for 2,000)	6,000
Balance at Bank	20,550	By Telephone Charges	540
To Subscriptions		By Electric Charges	250
(Including Rs. 750 for 2007)	21,250	By Stamp and Stationery	600
To Hall Rent	1,250	By Travelling	150
To Interest on Securities	1,000	By Donations	5,000
To Donations	10,000	By Meeting Expenses	500
To Telephone Receipts	50	By Rent	5,400
		By Library	3,000
		By Closing Balance :	
		Cash in hand	310
		Balance at Bank	32,600
	54,350		54,350

The Association also gives the following information :

(i) The Association holds 6% Govt. securities amounting to Rs. 40,000 on 1st January, 2006

(ii) The library account stood at Rs. 20,000 on 1.1.2006

(iii) Half of the donations is to be transferred to the Capital Fund.

(iv) Rent Rs. 300 is still payable.

18. Prepare an Income and Expenditure Account for the year ended 31st March, 2006 and the Balance Sheet as on that date of Modern College from the following :

Receipts and Payments Account
(for the year ended 31st March, 2006)

Receipts	Rs.	Payments	Rs.
To Cash on 1.4.05	20,000	By Pay and Allowances	70,500
To Tuition Fees	59,000	By Provident Fund Contribution	5,540
To Fines	1,000	By Printing & Stationery	700
To Grants from State Government	30,000	By Books for Library	4,600
To Interest Securities	300	By Postage & Telegram	500
To Rent from Use of Hall	1,000	By Newspapers etc.	300
		By Science Equipments	480
		By Laboratory Expenses	500
		By Construction of New Building	4,700
		By Repairs and Maintenance	600
		By Audit Fee	300
		By General Expenses	580
		By Cash on 31.3.2006	22,000
	1,11,300		1,11,300

The College had the following Assets as on 31st March 2005

Furniture Rs. 35,000, Land & Buildings Rs. 1,60,000, Library books Rs. 24,000, Investments Rs. 10,000, Outstanding Tuition Fee Rs. 2,200.

Provide for depreciation on the closing balances of the following assets :

Land and Buildings @ 5%, Furniture @15% and Library books @ 20%.

19. From the following receipts and payments account of a Sports Club and the additional information, prepare income and expenditure account for the year ended 31st Dec., 2006 and Balance Sheet as at that date :

Receipts	Rs.	Payments		Rs.
To Balance – Cash	352	By Crockery Purchased		265
To Current a/c with Cash	2,738	By Sundries		2,312
To Fixed Deposit at 6%	3,000	By Salaries		1,100
To Membership Subscriptions		By Postage Stamps		105
(Including Rs. 600 for 1997)	4,000	By Purchase of Cricket Goods		972
To Entrance Fees	275	By Investments		570
To Donations	501	By Tournament Expenses		1,880
To Interest on Fixed Deposit	90	By Upkeep of Lawn		400
To Tournament Fund	2,000	By Balance:		
To Sale of Crockery (Book value Rs. 120)	200	Cash in hand	220	
		Current a/c	2,332	
		Fixed Deposit	3,000	5,552
	13,156			13,156

Other Information :

(a) Monthly salary is Rs. 100.

(b) The value of unused postage stamps is as follows:

31st December, 2005 Rs. 75

31st December, 2006 Rs. 90

(c) Stock of cricket equipment is as follows:

31st December, 2005 Rs. 321

31st December, 2006 Rs. 280

(d) Arrear of membership subscription:

2005 Rs. 660

2006 Rs. 800

[Delhi, B. Com. (Pass), 1997 (B), Figures 10 times]

20. The following is the Receipts and Payments Account of Young Friend's Club in respect of the year ending 31st December, 2006:

Receipts		Rs.	Payment	Rs.
To Balance b/d		205	By Salaries	416
To Subscriptions:			By Stationery	80
2005	8		By Rates	120
2006	422		By Telephone	20
2007	16	446	By Investments	250
To Sports Meet Profit		310	By Sundry Expenses	185
To Dividends on Investments		200	By Balance c/d	90
		1,161		1,161

Other Information :

(i) There are 450 members each paying an annual subscription of Re. 1, Rs. 9 being in arrears for 2005.

(ii) Stock of stationery on 31st December, 2005 was Rs. 10 and 31st December 2006 Rs. 18.

(iii) In the books of the club building stands at Rs. 2000 and it is required to write off depreciation @ 5%.

Prepare the Club's Income and Expenditure a/c for the year ended 31st December, 2006 and the Balance Sheet as on that date.

[Delhi, B. Com. (Pass), 1990, 1991, 1992 (B)]

21. Following is the Receipts and Payments Account of Free Aid Medical Society for the year ended 31st March, 2006:

Receipts	Rs.	Payments	Rs.
To Cash on 1.4.05	7,000	By Payment for Medicines	30,000
To Subscriptions	50,000	By Honorarium to Doctors	10,000
To Donations	14,500	By Salaries	27,500
To Interest on Investment		By Sundry Expenses	500
@ 7% for the year	7,000	By Equipment	15,000
To Charity Show Proceeds	10,000	By Charity Show Expenses	1,000
		By Cash (Balance)	4,500
	88,500		88,500

Additional Information :

		On 31.3.2005	on 31.3.2006
(1)	Subscriptions due	500	1,000
(2)	Subscriptions received in advance	1,000	500
(3)	Stock of Medicine	10,000	15,000
(4)	Amount due to Medicine Suppliers	8,000	12,000
(5)	Value of Equipment	21,000	30,000
(6)	Value of Building	40,000	38,000

You are required to prepare (i) Income and Expenditure a/c for the year ended and (ii) Balance Sheet as on that date.

[Delhi, B. Com. (Pass) Examination 2000 (b)]

22. The Receipts and Payments Account and Income an Expenditure Account of a Club for the year ended 31st December, 2006 were as follows :

Receipts		Rs.	Payments	Rs.
To Balance b/d		1,500	By Books Purchased	1,000
To Subscriptions:			By Printing & Stationery	200
2005	600		By Salary	1,500
2006	4,300		By Advertisement	200
2007	200	5,100	By Electric Charges	400
To Interest on Investments		500	By Balance c/d	4,250
To Rent: 2005		150		
2006		300		
		7,550		7,550

Income and Expenditure Account

Expenditure	Rs.	Income	Rs.
To Salary	1,800	By Interest on Investment	400
To Tent Hire	200	By Subscriptions	4,800
To Electric Charges	400	By Rent	400
To Depreciation on Buildings	750		
To Depreciation on Furniture	100		
To Printing & Stationery	200		
To Advertisement	150		
To Surplus	2,000		
	5,600		5,600

The club assets on 1st January, 2006 were building Rs. 15,000, books Rs. 10,000, furniture Rs. 1,000, 4% investments Rs. 10,000, subscriptions in arrear at that date were Rs. 700. Liabilities on 1st January, 2006 were Rs. 50 for advertisement and Rs. 100 for salary.

You are required to prepare Balance Sheets of the club as at:

(i) December 31, 2005 and

(ii) December 31,2006.

23. The following particulars relate to Delhi Sports Club:

Income and Expenditure Account
(for the year ended 31st December, 2006)

Expenditure	Rs.	Income	Rs.
To Salaries	1,500	By Entrance Fees	10,500
To Stationery	2,200	By Subscriptions	15,600
To Advertising	1,600	By Rent	4,000
To Audit Fees	500		
To Fire Insurance	1,000		
To Depreciation on Sports Equipment	9,000		
To Excess of Income over Expenditure	14,300		
	30,100		30,100

Receipts and Payments Account
(for the year ended 31st December, 2006)

Receipts		Rs.	Payments		Rs.
To Balance b/d		4,200	By Salaries		1,000
To Entrance Fees		10,500	By Stationery:		
To Subscriptions:			2005	400	
2005	600		2006	2,200	2,600
2006	15,000		By Advertising		1,600
2007	400	16,000	By Fire Insurance		1,200
To Rent Received		3,500	By Investments		20,000
			By Balance c/d		7,800
		34,200			34,200

The assets on 1st January, 2006 included club grounds and pavilion Rs. 44,000. Sports equipments Rs. 25,000 and furniture Rs. 4,000. Subscriptions in arrears on that date were Rs. 800. Prepare :

(i) Balance Sheet as on 31st December, 2005

(ii) Balance Sheet as on 31st December, 2006

[Delhi, B. Com. (Pass), 1993 (modified);
Delhi, B. Com. (Hons.), 1984 1991 (modified)]

24. Following are the Receipts and Payments and Income and Expenditure Accounts of a Delhi Sports Club for the year ended on 31st December, 2006:

Income and Expenditure Account
(for the year ended 31st December, 2006)

Expenditure	Rs.	Income	Rs.
To Salaries	6,500	By Subscriptions	10,000
To Printing and Stationery	1,450	By Entrance Fees	2,500
To Audit Fees	250	By Sale of Newspapers	750
To Fire Insurance	750		
To Depreciation on Sports Equipments	2,700		
To Surplus (Excess of income Over expenditure	1,600		
	13,250		13,250

Receipts and Payments Account
(for the year ended 31st December, 2006)

Receipts		Rs.	Payments	Rs.
To Balance b/d		1,550	By Salaries	6,000
To Entrance Fees		2,500	By Printing and Stationery	1,200
To Subscriptions:			By Fire Insurance	1,000
2005	500		By Investment	5,000
2006	9,400		By Balance c/d	2,150
2007	800	10,700		
To Sale of Newspapers		600		
		15,350		15,350

Additional Information:

1. Subscriptions outstanding as on 31st December, 2005 amounting to Rs. 750.
2. Subscriptions outstanding as on 31st December, 2006 amounting to Rs. 600.
3. The assets of the Delhi Sports Club as on 1st January, 2006 were :
   Building Rs. 24,000, Sports Equipments Rs. 8,700, Furniture Rs. 5,400.
   You are required to prepare Balance Sheet as on 1st January, 2006 and 31st December, 2006

25. The following is the Income and Expenditure Account of Mumbai Swimming Club for the year ended 31st December, 2006

Expenditure	Rs.	Income	Rs
To Salaries	24,000	By Subscriptions	78,000
To Stationery	1,600	By Donations	8,000
To Postage, Telephone	3,200	By Billiard Table Collection	7,000
To Rates & Taxes	6,000	By Profit on Annual Meet	12,000
To Repairs	8,000	By Income from Investment	2,700
To Table Tennis balls	1,200		
To Printing of Souvenir	2,000		
To Electricity Charges	6,000		
To Billiard Room Expenses	3,000		
To Miscellaneous Expenses	9,400		
To Depreciation on Assets	2,000		
To Excess of Income over Expenditure	41,300		
	1,07,700		1,07,700

The following further information is available:

	1st Jan. 2006	31st Dec. 2006
	Rs.	Rs.
Assets	48,000	52,000
Outstanding Subscriptions	3,000	5,000
Advance Subscriptions	6,000	10,000
Expenses Outstanding:		
Stationery	600	400
Telephone	300	200
Electricity	700	300

Cash at Bank	1,800	?
Investment	27,000	47,000

From the foregoing, prepare a Receipts and Payments Account for the year 2006 and also draw the Balance Sheet as at 31st December, 2006.

26. The Income and Expenditure Account of the Old Ball and Bush Club for the year 2006 is as follows:

Expenditure	Rs.	Income	Rs.
To Salaries	47,500	By Subscriptions	75,000
To General Expenses	5,000	By Entrance Fees	2,500
To Audit Fee	2,500	By Contribution for Annual Dinner	10,000
To Secretary's Honorarium	10,000	By Profit on Annual Sports Meet	7,500
To Stationery & Printing	4,500		
To Annual Dinner Expenses	15,000		
To Interest & Bank Charges	1,500		
To Depreciation on Sports Equipment	3,000		
To Surplus	6,000		
	95,000		95,000

This account had been prepared after the following adjustments:

	Rs.
Subscriptions outstanding at the end of 2005	6,000
Subscriptions received in advance on 31st Dec., 2005	4,500
Subscriptions received in advance on 31st Dec., 2006	2,700
Subscriptions outstanding on 31st Dec. 2006	7,500

Salaries outstanding at the beginning of 2006 and the end of the 2006 were Rs. 4,000 and Rs. 4,500 respectively. General expenses include insurance prepaid to the extent of Rs. 600. Audit fees for 2005 are yet unpaid. During 2006 audit fees for 2005 amounting to Rs. 2,000 were paid.

The club owned a freehold ground valued at Rs. 1,00,000. The club has sports equipments on 1.1.2006 valued at Rs. 26,000. At the end of the year after depreciation, this equipment amounted to Rs. 27,000. In 2005 the club had raised a bank loan of Rs, 20,000. This was outstanding though 2006. On 31st Dec., 2006 Cash in hand amounted to Rs. 16,000.

Prepare the Receipts and Payments Account of the club for 2006 and the Balance Sheet as at 31st December, 2006.

27. From the following Income and Expenditure a/c and additional information, prepare the Receipts and Payments Account for the year ended 31st December 2006.

Income and Expenditure Account
(for the year ended 31st December, 2006)

Expenditure	Rs.	Income	Rs.
To Salaries	5,000	By Subscriptions	25,000
To Rent	3,000	By Donations	7,500
To Charities	1,200	By Profit on Sale of Assets	1,400
To Affiliation Fee to Rashtriya Club	500	By Miscellaneous Earnings	7,000
To Depreciation on Fixed Assets	1,600		
To Games & Sports	15,800		
To Periodicals	3,200		
To Sundry Expenses	1,900		
To Audit Fee	300		
To Excess of Income over Expenditure	8,400		
	40,900		40,900

Additional Information:

	31st Dec., 05	31st Dec., 06
	Rs.	Rs.
Marketable Securities	5,000	17,000
Outstanding Subscriptions	1,560	2,610
Prepaid Subscriptions	2,500	1,600
Deferred Salaries	600	700
Outstanding Sundry Expenses	1,300	1,500
Harijan Welfare Fund	15,000	18,000
Total depreciation upto the year ended	4,000	4,600
Fixed Assets (Original cost)	25,000	22,700
Debtors for Donations	1,500	4,500

During 2006 life membership fee collection is Rs. 12,400 and the expenses on Harijan Welfare amount to Rs. 9,500. Affiliation fee to the Rashtriya Club is advanced for 2006 and 2005 and Cash Balance is Rs. 11,150.

28. From the following particulars of star's cricket club, prepare an income and expenditure account for the year ending 31st December, 2005 and the Balance Sheet as at that date :

Receipts		Rs.	Payments	Rs.
To balance b/d		2,850	By Salaries	4,250
To Subscriptions			By Printing	2,450
2004	250		By Purchase of Investments	8,000
2005	8,950		By Expenditure on refreshments	4,200
2006	550	9,750	By Payments of expenses of last year	340
To Donation for Cricket pavilion		6,000	By Additions to club building	4,000
To Sale of furniture		300	By Cost of Gold Medal	175
To Interest on investment		1,200	By Balance c/d	2,285
To Sale of refreshments		5,600		
		25,700		25,700

In addition to the above, the following further details are available from the accounts of the club.

(i) The assets on 1st January 2005 include club buildings Rs. 15,000, Investments Rs. 6,000 and furniture Rs. 2000. The liabilities as on 1st January 2005 include an account styled cricket prizes fund account Rs. 5000.

(ii) of interest on investments Rs. 150 pertains to the last year and Rs. 320 is still owing.

(iii) Stock of refreshment at the end of the year was valued at Rs. 55.

(iv) The cricket prize fund was not separately invested. It was decided to set apart every year Rs. 200 from the interest income of the club to be utilized for the purpose of awarding a gold medal to the best cricketer of the year.

[Delhi, B. Com (Hons) I year 2004]

ANSWER

B. Objective Type Question

I. (1) F (2) F

II. (1) II , (2) iii (3) ii

C. Exercises

1. Rs. 1,300 (Payment on account of salary during the year)
2. Stationery consumed. Rs. 4,150
3. (i) Subscriptions shown in a/c 6,650
   (ii) B/S

Liabilities	Rs.	Assets	Rs.
Subscriptions Received in advance	600	Subscriptions	300
		o/s ford for 05	1250

		Rs.
4.	Amount of stationery used	
	To be shown in Income & Expenditure a/c	3,700
5.	(i) Amount of donations to be shown is Income & Expenditure a/c	3,750
	(ii) Donations o/s for 2006	1,750
6.	Salaries received during the year	2,300
7.	(i) Subscriptions to be shown in Income & Expenditure	52,500

Liabilities	Rs.	Assets	Rs
Sub Reed in advance	1,500	Subscription o/s	8000

			Rs.
8.	(i)	Surplus	565
	(ii)	Total of B/S	4,019
	(iii)	Opening capital fund	3,144
9.	(i)	Surplus	8,501
	(ii)	Total of B/S	39,779
	(iii)	opening capital funds	29,808
10.	(i)	Surplus	2,235
	(ii)	Total of Balance sheet	8,420
	(iii)	Opening capital fund	6,075
11.	(i)	Surplus	3,560
	(ii)	Total of Balance Sheet	42,480
12.	(i)	Deficit	630
	(ii)	Total of opening B/S	25,260
	(iii)	Total of closing B/S	36,430
13.	(i)	Surplus	4,48,000
	(ii)	Total of Balance Sheet	29,83,000
14.	(i)	Surplus	14,150
	(ii)	Total of Balance Sheet	53,040
		Hint - opening capital funds	36,000
15.	(i)	Surplus	2,566
	(ii)	Total of Balance Sheet	9,866

16.	(i)	Surplus	2,615
	(ii)	Total of Balance Sheet	17,945
	(iii)	Opening Capital Fund	15,170
17.	(i)	Surplus	10,860
	(ii)	Capital Fund at the beginning	80,800
	(iii)	Total of Balance Sheet	97,710
18.	(i)	Deficit [Excess of Expenditure over income	9,625
	(ii)	Total of Balance Sheet	2,41,575
19.	(i)	Deficit [Excess of Expenditure over Income]	555
	(ii)	Total of Balance Sheet	7,707
20.	(i)	Surplus	47
	(ii)	Total of Balance Sheet	2,287
21.	(i)	Deficit	8,000
	(ii)	Total of Balance Sheet	1,88,500
	(iii)	Opening Capital Fund	1,69,500
22.	(i)	Opening Balance Sheet	38,450
	(ii)	Closing Balance Sheet	41,100
	(iii)	Opening Capital Fund	38,300
23.	(i)	Total of Opening Balance Sheet	78,000
	(ii)	Total of Closing Balance Sheet	93,300
24.	(i)	Total of Balance Sheet on 31.12.06	40,400
	(ii)	Total of Balance Sheet as on 31.12.06	43,800
25.	(i)	Cash at Bank (closing balance)	20,400
	(ii)	Subscription Receipts	80,000
	(iii)	Capital Fund in the beginning	72,200
	(iv)	Total of Balance Sheet	1,24,400
26.	(i)	Cash at Bank (opening balance)	13,900
	(ii)	Total of receipts and payments a/c	1,05,600
	(iii)	Total of balance sheet	1,51,100
27.	(i)	Opening Cash Balance	600
	(ii)	Total of receipts and payments a/c	63,750
28.	(i)	Surplus	4,875

Hint-if book value of furniture sold is taken Rs. 300, otherwise the above figure may be reduced by Rs. 1,700 if it is treated as a loss on furniture.

(ii)	Opening Capital Fund	20,910
(iii)	Total of Closing Balance Sheet (if book value of furniture is taken as Rs. 1,700)	37,360

CHAPTER 14

ACCOUNTS FROM INCOMPLETE RECORDS SINGLE ENTRY SYSTEM

A. Essay type questions

1. What do you understand by single entry system? Discuss its merits and limitations.
2. Discuss the merits of single entry system. Is there any limitation of this system? If yes, then explain.
[Delhi, B. Com. (Pass) 1999, 2001 (B)]
3. Distinguish between-
(i) Statement of affairs and Balance Sheet
[Delhi, B.com. (Pass 1996, 1999 A & B), 2006 (B)]
(ii) Single Entry System and Double Entry System of accounting.
[Delhi, B.Com. (Pass) 1995, 1999 (B)]
4. Write short notes on the following:
(i) Defects of single entry system.
[Delhi, B.Com. (Pass) 1994]
(ii) Methods of calculating profits under Single Entry System:
[Delhi B.Com. (Hons.) I yr. 2000, Delhi B Com. (Pass) 2005B]
5. How single entry system is converted into double entry system? Explain.

B) Objective type questions:-

1. Do you agree with the following statements?
(i) Single Entry system is a scientific system.
(ii) It is used by big business houses.
(iii) It is incomplete system.
(iv) It is used by small traders only.
2. Indicate the correct answer.
(i) Single Entry system contains
(a) All the relevant accounts
(b) Only personal accounts.
(c) Real accounts only.
(d) Personal account and cash book.
(ii) Credit sales can be ascertained by preparing-
(a) Total creditors a/c
(b) Total debtors a/c
(c) None of the above.
(iii) Opening Balance of creditors can be calculated by preparing-
(a) Total debtors a/c
(b) Bills payable a/c
(c) Total creditors a/c
(d) None of the above
(iv) Cash balance either opening or closing can be ascertained by making-
(a) Trading a/c
(b) Total debtors a/c
(c) Cash a/c
(d) None of the above

(v) Bill dishonoured is shown

(a) Bills Receivable a/c

(b) Bills Receivable a/c and Debtor a/c

(c) Debtors a/c

(d) None of the above.

Exercises

1. Calculate capital at the end from the following!

	Rs.
Sundry debtors	2700
Stock	12,300
Furniture & fixture	5,450
Rent Accrued	500
Sundry creditors	12,000
Expenses owing for salaries	250

2. X, who keeps his books on single entry, tells you that his capital on 31st December, 2006 was Rs. 18,700 and capital on 1st January, 2006 was Rs. 19,200. He further informs you that during the year he withdrew for his household purposes RS. 8,420. He once sold his investment of Rs. 5000 at 5% premium and brought that money into the business.
You are required to calculate his profit or loss during the period.

3. Mr. Roop started a business on 1st January 2006, with a capital of Rs. 25,000. On 1st April he borrowed from his uncle a sum of Rs. 10,000 on 31st December 2006, his position was-

Cash in hand	Rs. 2000
Debtors	25,500
Stock	17,800
Sundry creditors	3,750
Drawings	5,000

Calculate his profit or loss during the period.

4. The following are the details as on 1st January 2006 regarding the business affairs of Mr. Rakesh who maintains accounts on single entry system-

	Rs.
Cash in hand	300
Cash at Bank	5,500
Stock	6,600
Debtors	3,457
Creditors	4,557
Furniture	1,000

His position at the end of the year was as follows:

	Rs.
Cash in hand	380
Cash at Bank	2,400
Stock	5,680

Debtors	4,620
Furniture	1,250
Sundry creditors	3,500

During the year, he withdrew Rs. 7,500 out of which he purchased a scooter for Rs. 5,000.

Prepare a statement showing his business results.

5. Calculate the amount of cash received from debtors during the year.

		Rs.
1.	Debtors as on 1.1.06	60,000
2.	Credit sales	5,40,000
3.	Bad debts during the year	5,000
4.	Returns from debtors	15,000
5.	Debtors as on 31.12.06	30,000

6. Calculate the amount of cash paid to the creditors during the year:

		Rs.
1.	Creditors as on 1.1.06	45,000
2.	Credit Purchases	2,50,000
3.	Cash purchases	14,000
4.	Returns	5,000
5.	Creditors as on 31.12.06	57,000

7. Madhu maintains books on single entry system. He gives you the following information:

Capital as on January1, 2005 Rs. 15,200

Capital as on January 1, 2006 Rs. 16,900

Drawings made during the period January 1, 2005 to January 2006 Rs. 4,800

Capital introduced on August 1, 2005 Rs. 2,000

You are required to calculate profit made by Madhu,

8. From the following particulars, prepare Bills Receivable Account and Total Debtors Account for the year ended 31st December, 2006

Particulars	*Rs.*	*Particulars*	*Rs.*
Total Debtors on 1.1.06	36,000	Returns inwards	15,000
Bills Receivable on 1.1.06	10,000	Discount allowed to Debtors	10,000
Sales (including cash sales Rs. 20,000) made during year	3,00,000	Bad debts written off	3,000
		Bill Receivable endorsed to crs.	10,000
Cash received from Debtors	2,00,000	Cash received on Bill matured	15,000
Bills Receivable on 31.12.06	15,000		

9. Prepare the total debtors and total creditors Accounts and find out the amount of sales and purchases from the following particulars:

From Cash Book	*Rs.*
Cash received from debtors	75,000
Cash paid to creditors	44,000
Cash purchases	12,500
Cash sales	20,000
Discount received	3,000
Discount paid	4,000

From Personal Ledger	Debtors Rs.	Creditors Rs.
Opening Balance	60,000	24,000
Closing Balance	65,000	20,000
Bills Receivable	3,000	-
Bills Payable	-	4,000
Bad debts	2,000	-

10. From the following facts supplied by a businessman who keeps his book on single entry. You are required to calculate total sales.

		Rs.
(1)	Opening Balance of Debtors as on 1.1.2006	9,000
(2)	Closing Balance of Debtors as on 31.12.2006	12,500
(3)	Cash received from debtors during the year	30,500
(4)	Discount Allowed	50
(5)	Returns inwards	400
(6)	Cash Sales	23,100
(7)	Bad debts during the year	200

11. From the following information, you are required to calculate total purchases:

		Rs.
(1)	Opening Balance of Creditors	7,500
(2)	Closing Balance of Creditors	26,000
(3)	Cash paid to Creditors	37,500
(4)	Cash Purchases	24,000
(5)	Returns outwards	1,000

12. Mr. Manish tells you that his capital on 31st December, 2006 is RS, 18,700 and his capital on 1st January, 2006 was Rs. 19,200. He further informs you that during the year he gave loan of Rs. 3,500 to his brother on private account and withdrew Rs. 300 per months for personal purposes. He also used a flat for his personal purposes, the rent of which at the rate of Rs. 100 p.m. and electricity charges as an average of Rs.10 p.m. were paid from the business account. He once sold his 7% Government bond Rs. 2,000 at 2% premium and brought that money into the business. Besides, this is no other information.

You are required to prepare a statement of profit.

13. M. Nishar carries on a grocery business and does not keep his books on double entry basis. The following particulars have been extracted from his books:

Particulars	1.7.2005 (Rs.)	30.6.2006 (Rs.)
Plant & Machinery	25,000	25,000
Stock	22,000	19,500
Sundry Debtors	8,000	25,500
Sundry Creditors	12,500	10,000
Cash in hand	400	800
Bank Balance	(Dr.) 6,250	(Cr.) 7,000

The following transactions appear in the cash book of the year.

Received on account of cash sales Rs. 31,250, Received from sundry debtors Rs. 1,60,000, payment for purchases Rs. 28,850, payment to Sundry Creditors Rs, 1,32,000. General expenses of the business Rs. 21,450, Wages paid Rs. 15,000 and drawings Rs. 6,800.

During the year Nishar has taken goods worth Rs. 1,950 from the business for his own use and has not paid any amount into the business for them.

Prepare P & L a/c for the year ending 30th June 2006 after charging 10% depreciation on plant and Machinery and the balance sheet of the same year.

14. Mohit did not keep proper books of accounts. However, he gave you the following information relating to 2006:

Assets and Liabilities	*As on 1.1.06 (Rs.)*	*As on 31.12.06 (Rs.)*
Cash at Bank	1,000	1,800
Stock	20,000	19,500
Debtors	15,000	16,000
Machinery	40,000	-
Sundry Creditors	20,000	18,500

Summary of Cash Transactions:

Receipts	*Rs.*	*Payment*	*Rs.*
Opening Balance	1,000	Payment to Creditors	35,000
Received from Debtors	76,500	Wages	15,100
Cash sales	8,200	Salaries	11,600
Sales of Old Newspaper	200	Building	20,000
Loan from Mrs. Mohit @ 9% on 1.1.2006		Drawing	8,400
	6,000	Closing Balance	1,800
	91,900		91,900

During the year Rs. 600 had to be written off as bad. Machinery is to be depreciated @ 15% p.a. Expenses owing are Rs. 800.

Prepare Trading a/c, Profit & loss a/c for the year ending on 31.12.06 and Balance Sheet as on 31.12.06

15. Roshan Washing House is owned by Roshan. He keeps his books on single entry. He gives you the following information:

Particulars	*Dec. 31, 05 (Rs.)*	*Dec 31. 06 (Rs.)*
Furniture and Fittings	5,000	6,000
Stock of Materials	3,000	1,000
Sundry Debtors	6,000	7,000
Sundry Creditors	2,000	NIL
Prepaid Expenses	NIL	200
Unpaid Expenses	600	1,000
Cash in hand	1,100	300

Receipts and Payments during the year:	Rs.
Receipt from Debtors	21,000
Paid to Creditors	10,000
Cartage	2,000
Drawings	12,000
Sundry Expenses	16,000
Furniture purchases for cash	1,000

Prepare a Trading and Profit & Loss Account for the year ended Dec. 31, 2006 and a Balance Sheet after providing for bad debts at 10%. There was a considerable amount of cash sales.

16. Following is the position of assets and liabilities of Shri Vishal who maintains his books on single entry system:

Particulars	*1st Jan 06 Rs.*	*31st Dec 06 Rs.*
Debtors	1,06,000	1,79,000
Creditors	30,000	39,000
Stock	34,000	38,000
Fixed Assets	42,800	34,800

Other information are as follows:	Rs.
Total Sales (including Cash Sales Rs. 10,000)	2,00,000
Total Purchases (Including Cash Purchases Rs. 41,000)	90,000
General Business Expenses	20,000
Drawings	6,000
Cash in hand and at Bank	8,200
Payment for fixed assets	10,000

The proprietor has taken out goods worth Rs. 10,000 for his private use and goods worth Rs. 1,000 have been used in the construction of a part of plant. Interest on Capital is allowed at 5%.

You are required to prepare Trading and Profit & Loss A/c and Balance Sheet from the information given above.

17. A trader has not kept complete records of his business transactions for the year 2006 (that is, he has adopted so called single entry system of book-keeping). The following facts relating to his business are, however, available:

a. **The summary of his cash book:** Cash paid into bank Rs. 8,690. Dividends received in cash Rs. 200. Drawings in cash Rs. 445 and out of bank Rs. 750. Cash received from debtors Rs. 11,700, payments to creditors by cash Rs. 200 and by cheques Rs. 7,750. Wages paid in cash Rs. 1,500. Sundry expenses paid in cash Rs. 1,075. Bank interest received Rs. 10.

b. **His assets and liabilities were:**

Particulars	*1st Jan 2006 Rs.*	*31st Dec 2006 Rs.*
Stock	600	750
Bank Balance	800	1,000
Cash in hand	30	20
Debtors	750	1,050
Creditors	1,200	1,400
Investments	3,000	3,000

From the foregoing information, prepare his cash book and the Trading and Profit & Loss A/c for the year ended December 31st 2006 and his Balance Sheet as at that date bearing in mind that Sundry Expenses amounting to Rs. 120 were outstanding at the end of the year.

18. Manoj commenced business as a cloth merchant on 1st Jan., 2006 with a capital of Rs. 2,000. On the same day, he purchased furniture for cash Rs. 600. He keeps his books under single entry system.

From the following particulars prepare trading and Profit & Loss a/c for the year ended 31st December 2006 and a balance sheet as on that date:

	Rs.
Sales (including cash also Rs. 1,400)	3,400
Purchases (including cash purchases of Rs. 800)	3,000
Manoj's Drawings	240
Salaries	400
Bad debts written off	100
Business Expenses	140
Stock of Goods on 31,12,06	1,300
Debtors on 31.12.06	1,040
Creditors on 31.12.06	720

Manoj took cloth worth Rs. 100 form the shop for private use and paid Rs. 60 cash to his son but forgot to record these transactions in his books. Provide depreciation on furniture at 10 p.c.

19. The following information is extracted from the incomplete records of the partnership of the Hussain and Rajan:

Particulars	*1st Jan 2006 Rs.*	*31st Dec 2006 Rs.*
Machinery	1,000	-
Furniture	7,500	-
Stock	11,275	10,180
Debtors	12,750	-
Cash	1,975	3,535
Creditors	-	6,370

Purchases and sales during the year amounted to Rs. 61,510 and Rs. 80,190 respectively and compared to Husains's capital Rajan's capital is more by Rs. 5,000 as at 1st Jan., 2006. Cash transactions during the year were as follows:

Receipts	*Rs.*	*Payments*	*Rs.*
To Trade Customers	72,740	By suppliers	63,960
To Hussain's capital	5,000	By Salaries	8,750
(additional)		By Rent (For 6 months) up to 30.6.2006	3,000
		By Rates and taxes	
		(For 6 months up to 31.3.2007)	3,000
		By Electric charges	1,250
		By Advertising	870
		By Delivery Charges	680
		By Repairs	1,810
		By Sundry Expenses	700
		By Drawings Hussain	2,760
		By Rajan	2,125

On 31st December 2006, outstanding liabilities also included: Electricity Charges Rs. 260, Advertising Rs. 130, and Sundry Expenses Rs. 200.

Depreciate Furniture and Machinery by 5% and 20% respectively. Provide 4% for bad debts. Cash purchases are not made.

Prepare final Accounts for the year ended 31st December, 2006

20. Ding and Dong are partners in a firm Ding Dong to, which does not maintain its books of account properly. The partners share profits and losses in the ratio 3:2 and Balance Sheet from the information given below:

(a) Cash and Bank Transactions:	Rs.
Bank balance as on 1.1.06	2,400
Received form Debtors	38,000
Cash sales	9,400
Paid to creditors	22,800
Wages	5,000
Salaries	4,600
Sundry expenses	7,800
Ding's drawings	4,400
Don's drawings	3,300
Cash in hand on 31.12.2006	120
Cash in Bank on 31.12.2006	1,930

(b) The Capitals of Ding And Dong on 1st January 2006 were Rs. 16,000 and Rs. 14,550 respectively. The assets and liabilities of the firm were:

Particulars	*1st Jan 2006 Rs.*	*31st Dec., 2006 Rs.*
Motor car	12,000	12,000
Furniture	1,200	1,200
Stock	11,800	15,000
Debtors	18,000	15,000
Creditors	15,000	16,200

21. Mr. Young keeps his books on single entry system. From the following prepare trading and profit & loss Account for the year ended 31st March 2006 together with balance sheet as at that date.

Cash Book

Date	*Particulars*	*Rs.*	*Date*	*Particulars*	*Rs.*
2006			2005		
March 31	To Debtors	25,000	April 05	By Bank overdraft	4,000
March 31	To sales	15,000	2006	By interest	100
			March 31	By drawings	2,000
				By Salaries	8,500
				By Expenses	7,900
				By Creditors	15,000
				By Balance c/d Bank	2,425
				Cash	75
		40,000			40,000

Further details are available:

Assets & Liabilities	*Rs.* 1.4.2005	*Rs.* 31.3.2006
Stock in hand	9,000	10,220
Creditors	8,000	5,500
Debtors	22,000	30,000
Furniture	1,000	1,000
Office Premises	15,000	15,000

Provide 5 per cent interest on Young's capital on 1.4.2005, provide Rs. 1,500 for doubtful debts 5 per cent depreciation on fixed assets, 5 percent group commission as Incentive to staff has to be provided for on net profit after meeting all expenses and the commission.

22. Mr. K.K. Gupta who has not kept a complete set of books, asks you to prepare his final accounts for the year ended 31st Dec., 2006. You are, however, able to obtain the following information:

Summary of cash book:

Balance of cash on 1st Jan., 2006 Rs. 5,170, Receipt from debtors Rs. 42,050, personal drawings Rs. 3,000. Payments to creditors Rs. 32,400. Salaries Rs. 2,500, Rent Rs. 1,200, Electricity charges Rs. 350, Printing and Stationery Rs. 210, and Advertising Rs. 450.

His other assets and liabilities were:

Particulars	*31st Dec., 2005 Rs.*	*31st Dec. 2006 Rs.*
Debtors	3,350	5,100
Creditors	1,400	3,500
Rent outstanding	100	100
Electricity charges outstanding	20	10
Advertising outstanding	-	250

The stock on 31st Dec., 2006 was valued at Rs. 4,500, but the trader has no record of the opening stock. He informs you, however, that he invariably sold his goods at cost plus 33 1/3%.

Prepare his profit & loss A/c for the year ended 31st Dec., 2006 and his Balance Sheet as on that date.

23. Sanchit commenced business on 1st April 2005 with a capital of Rs. 20,000. On the same day he purchased furniture for Rs. 4,000. From the following particulars obtained from his books, which don't conform to strict double entry principles, you are required to prepare Trading and profit & loss A/c and Balance Sheet for the year ended 31st March, 2006

	Rs.
Sales (including Cash Sales Rs. 10,000)	25,000
Purchases (including Cash Purchases Rs. 6,000)	20,000
Sanchit's drawings	1,000
Salaries to staff	2,400
Bad debts written off	200
Trading Expenses	800

Sanchit has used cloth worth RS. 600 for his private purpose and paid Rs. 1,000 to his son which is not recorded any where on 31st March, 2006, his debtors were worth Rs. 7,000 and creditors Rs. 4,000, stock in trade on that date was worth RS. 8,000.

24. Mahesh chandra is owner of a shop of General Merchandise. He maintains his accounts on single entry system. He wants to know the result of his business on 31st December, and for that following information's are available:

Particulars	*1.1.2005 Rs.*	*31.12.2006 Rs.*
Cash	150	175
Bank Balance	750	800
Furniture	100	100
Stock	500	650
Creditors	350	400
Debtors	250	300

During the year he had withdrawn Rs. 500 for his personal use and invested Rs. 250 as additional capital. Calculate his Profit on 31st Dec., 2006 and prepare statement of affairs as on that date.

25. M/s. V.I.P. Hoisery, Ludhiana have only a Bank Pass Book and does not keep any other book of accounts. From the following informations, prepare his final account of the year ended 31st Dec., 2006.

An analysis of the Pass Book shows:

Total amount received from Debtors and deposited with the Bank Rs. 74,100, Drawings Rs. 6,000, Payments to creditors Rs. 40,800, Salaries Rs. 3,000, Advertisement Expenses Rs. 900, Sundry Trade Expenses 3,600, Charity Rs. 2,400, Income Tax Rs. 600, Building Rs. 20,000 and Balance at Bank on 31.12.06 Rs. 5,000.

An amount of Rs. 9,350 is outstanding in respect of sales of 2006. In additional there are four Bills receivable amounting in all Rs. 850, which are irrecoverable. His liabilities were as under:

Particulars	*As on 31.12.2005 Rs.*	*As on 31.12.06 Rs.*
Creditors	4,800	7,000
Advertisement Expenses	-	500
Salaries	400	500

The estimated value of stock in trade on 31.12.2006 is Rs. 7,000, but no information is available regarding the stock in trade on 31.12.2005. The trader takes 25% profit on sales.

Give important notes to show how you have arranged at the unknown figures.

26. The Balance Sheet of C. Raja as on 31st Dec., 2006 was as follows:

Liabilities	*Amount Rs.*	*Assets*	*Amount Rs.*
Creditors	36,050	Freehold Premises	78,000
Capital	1,67,700	Plant & Machinery	21,000
		Furniture & Fittings	10,200
		Stock	43,800
		Debtors	49,100
		Cash	1,650

Raja maintained only a cash Book and a Ledger. The summary of his Receipts and payments for the year ended on 31st Dec., 2006 is given below:

Receipts	*Rs.*	*Payments*	*Rs.*
To Cash sales	93,150	By Cash Purchases	25,000
To Cash from credit sales	2,13,800	By Creditors for goods purchased	1,72,700
Capital introduced	10,000	By Wages	37,150
		By General expenses	31,350
		By Addition to plant & Machinery	6,400
		By Addition to Furniture	1,600
		By Drawings	26,800

As on 31.12.06 the amount due from Debtors was Rs. 45,900 and the amount due to creditors was Rs. 40,800, liability for expenses was Rs. 2,550 and the value of stock was Rs. 42,700 as on that date.

You are required to prepare the Trading and Profit & Loss Account of C. Raja for the year ended 31st December, 2006 and the Balance Sheet as on that date after making adjustments in respect of the following:

(i) Depreciation at 10% is to be provided on Plant and Machinery and on Furniture & fittings.

(ii) Rs, 7,500 to be provided for bad debts.

(iii) Goods supplied to the proprietor for his private purpose Rs. 1,900 was included in the Debtors balances as on 31.12.2006

(iv) Sales Returns amounted Rs 6600

27. A trader keeps his books by single entry. During the year 2006, he kept a cash Book of which the following is an analysis-

	Rs.
Received form debtors	64,000
Additional capital introduced on 1st Oct. 2006	8,000
Loan from Z @ 10% p.a. On 1st July 2006	10,500
Paid to Sundry creditors	57,700
General Expenses paid	3,900
Salaries paid	3,000
Drawings	4,000
Deposits in the Bank during the year	50,000
Withdrawals from Bank during the year	36,000

The following balances existed on 1st Jan 2006 Sundry debtors Rs 15,300, Sundry Creditors Rs, 11,500 Bank overdraft Rs. 8,000, Buildings 42,500, stock Rs. 21,800 and cash Balance Rs. 600.

The following balances existed on 31st Dec 06 Sundry debtors Rs. 16000, Sundry creditors 11,900 and stock Rs. 26,000.

Depreciate buildings by 5% and provide interest on Z's loan.

Prepare trading and profit and loss a/c for the year ended 31st December 2006 and a balance Sheet as on that date. Give all working neatly and clearly.

28. Following figures were extracted from the books of X

	Rs.
Sales (inclusive of cash Rs. 8,000)	20,000
Purchases (inclusive of cash Rs. 2500)	12,000
Bad debts written off	750
Business Expenses	1,050

X who started his business on 1st Jan 06 with a capital of Rs, 10,000, spent Rs. 1500 on furniture immediately. During the year he took goods worth Rs. 1500 and withdrew Rs. 1300 as cash for his personal use.

The position on 31st Dec, 2006 as	Rs.
Stock	1,500
Debtors	1,250
Creditors	1,500

Prepare his final accounts.

ANSWER

B. Object type questions

1. (i) No. (ii) No. (iii) Yes (iv) Yes
2. (i) (d) (ii) (b) (iii) (c) (iv) (c) (v) (b)

C. Exercises

			Rs.
1.		Capital at the end	14,250
2.		Profit during the year	2,670
3.		Profit	11,550
4.		Profit	6,030
5.		Cash Received	5,00,000
6.		Cash paid to creditors	2,33,000
7.		profit made during the year	4,500
8.	(i)	Amount of sales	58,000
	(ii)	Bills Received	30,000
9.	(i)	Amount of sales (Credit Sales Rs. 89,000)	1,09,000
	(ii)	Amount of purchases (Credit purchases Rs. 47,000)	59,500
10.	(i)	Total sales (Credit purchases Rs. 34,650)	57,750
11.	(i)	Total Purchases (Credit purchases Rs. 57,000)	81,000
12.		Profit	5,880
13.	(i)	Net Profit	10,900
	(ii)	Total of Balance Sheet	68,300
	(iii)	Drawings deductible	8750
14.	(i)	Gross profit	37,200
	(ii)	Net Profit	18,265
	(iii)	Total of balance sheet	91,300
	(iv)	Credit sales	78,100
	(v)	Credit purchases	33,500
15.	(i)	Gross profit	29,200
	(ii)	Net profit	12,300
	(iii)	Total of Balance Sheet	13,800
	(iv)	Total sales (including credit sales Rs, 22,000)	41,200
	(v)	Purchases	8,000
	(vi)	Capital in the beginning	12,500
16.	(i)	Gross Profit	1,25,000
	(ii)	Net profit	77,950
	(iii)	Total of Balance sheet	2,70,000
	(iv)	Capital at the beginning	1,61,000
	(v)	Cash at the end	21,200
17.	(i)	Gross Profit	2,500
	(ii)	Net Profit	1,515
	(iii)	Total of Balance Sheet	5,820
	(iv)	Capital- Opening	3,980
		Closing	4,300
	(v)	Credit sales	12,000
	(vi)	Credit purchases	8,150

18.	(i)	Gross Profit	1,800
	(ii)	Net Profit	1,100
	(iii)	Total of Balance Sheet	3,420
	(iv)	Cash Balance at the end	540
	(v)	Collection from debtors	860
	(v)	Payment to creditors	1,480
19.	(i)	Gross profit	17,585
	(ii)	Net Loss	5,439
	(iii)	Total of Balance Sheet	30,316
	(iv)	Debtors at the beginning	7,475
	(v)	creditors at the beginning	8,820
	(vi)	Cash sales ascertained form cash book.	12,725
20.	(i)	Gross profit	18,600
	(ii)	Net Profit-Ding	2,011
	Dong		1,341
	(iii)	Total of Balance Sheet	43,930
	(iv)	Purchases	24,000
	(v)	Credit Sales	35,000
21.	(i)	Gross profit	36,720
	(ii)	Net Profit	15,400
	(iii)	Total of Balance Sheet	56,420
	(iv)	Credit purchases	12,500
	(v)	Credit Sales	33,000
	(iv)	Capital (a) opening	35,000
		(b) Closing	50,150
22.	(i)	Gross profit	10,950
	(ii)	Net profit	6,000
	(iii)	Total of Balance Sheet	16,750
	(iv)	Value of opening stock	2,850
	(v)	Closing cash Balance	7,110
23.	(i)	Gross Profit	13,600
	(ii)	Net Profit	10,200
	(iii)	Total of Balance Sheet	31,600
24.	(i)	Profit	475
	(ii)	Total of Statement of Affairs	2,025
25.	(i)	Gross Profit	21,075
	(ii)	Net Profit	9,125
	(iii)	Total of Balance Sheet	41,350
	(iv)	Value of opening stock	27,225
26.	(i)	Gross profit	63,050
	(ii)	Net Profit	17,730

	(iii)	Credit sales	2,17,200
	(iv)	Credit Purchases	1,77,450
	(v)	Total of Balance Sheet	2,10,080
27.	(i)	Gross Profit	10,800
	(ii)	Net Profit	1,250
	(iii)	Total of Balance Sheet	88,875
	(iv)	Cash in hand at the end	500
	(v)	Cash at Bank at the end	6,000
28.	(i)	Gross Profit	11,000
	(ii)	Net Profit	9,200
	(iii)	Total of Balance Sheet	17,900
	(iv)	Closing cash in hand	13,650

CHAPTER 15

CONSIGNMENT ACCOUNT

A. Essay Type Questions

1. What is consignment? Explain
2. Distinguish between -
   (i) Consignment and sale ([Delhi, B.Com (Pass) 2001 (B)])
   (ii) Consignment and Joint Venture ([Delhi, B.Com (Pass) 1995, 1999 (B), 2006(B)])
   (iii) Del-credere and overriding commission. [Delhi, B.Com (Pass) 2005]
   (iv) General and Del-credere commission.
   (v) Normal and Abnormal losses. [Delhi, B.Com (Pass) 1995]
3. Describe the method of determining the value of unsold stock of goods sent on consignment. [Delhi, B.Com (Pass) 1993, 1996]
4. Write short notes on:
   (a) Del-credere commission [Delhi, B.Com (Pass) 2001]
   (b) Over riding commission [Delhi, B.Com (Pass) 1993,2002 (B)]
   (c) Abnormal loss [Delhi, B.Com. (Pass) 2006 (B)]

B. Objective Type Questions

1) Indicate the correct answers of the following:
   (a) Consignment is
      (i) a Personal a/c
      (ii) a Real a/c
      (iii) a Nominal a/c
   (b) Del-credere commission is paid
      (i) when sales are there
      (ii) when credit sales are there
      (iii) when there is a bad debt and the consignee agrees to pay.
   (c) Over riding commission is payable
      (i) when sales are of normal price
      (ii) when sales are of invoice price
      (iii) when sales are more than invoice price.
   (d) The Abnormal loss is credited to
      (i) Normal loss a/c i.e. consignment a/c
      (ii) Abnormal loss a/c i.e. P & L a/c
      (iii) Difficult to say
   (e) Unsold stock is valued at cost or at invoice price along with proportionate expenses which are-
      (i) recurring nature
      (ii) non-recurring nature
      (iii) no such distinction is taken.

2. State whether the following statements are true or false.
   (i) Sales Account and Account Sales are synonymous.
   (ii) Overriding commission is paid when the consignee agrees to bear the loss on account of bad debts.
   (iii) Del-credere commission is the difference between actual sale price and invoice price.
   (iv) Proportionate share of non-recurring expenses is added in the valuation of unsold stock lying with the consignee.
   (v) Abnormal loss arises in the normal circumstances.
   (vi) Sale is there when goods are sent on consignment.
   (vii) Ownership passes immediately when goods are sent on consignment

C. Exercises

1. R of Mumbai consigned 100 bags of goods costing Rs. 600 each of Prashant of Sri Ganga Nagar. The consignor sent the goods at a pro-forma invoice price of 25% above cost to the consignee. R spent Rs. 1,600 on packing, while taking delivery of the goods, Prashant paid Rs. 1,900 as freight and cartage. Prashant sold 80 bags @ 820 per bag. He paid Rs. 2,200 as godown rent. Prashant is to get a commission of 5% on sales.

   Prepare consignment account and Prashant's account in the books of R.

2. A of Delhi sent on consignment goods to B of Mumbai at a cost of Rs. 59,350. A paid for freight Rs. 1,988 and insurance Rs. 1,400. Half of the goods were sold by the consignee for Rs. 35,000. B is entitled to a commission of Rs. 1,750. Godown expenses of Rs. 400 and selling expenses of Rs. 700. One-fourth of the consignment was lost by fire. A claim of Rs. 10,000 was recovered. Draw up ledger accounts in the books of A.

   [Delhi, B.Com. (Pass), 1989 (Correspondence Courses)]

3. M/s Gupta Traders of Delhi sent 100 sewing machines on consignment to G. Prasad of Patna. Each machine costs Rs. 200. The consignor paid Rs. 1,000 by way of freight and insurance etc. G Prasad spent Rs. 500 by way of godown rent and other expenses. At the end of the year 10 machines remaining unsold with G. Prasad. The consignee sold sewing machines @ Rs. 250 per machine. G. Prasad remitted the sale proceeds after deducting expenses and his commission which was 5% of the goods sold.

   Prepare a Consignment to Patna a/c and G. Prasad's a/c in the books of M/s. Gupta Traders, Delhi.

4. A consigns to B 100 bags of sugar, costing Rs. 300 each. He pays Rs. 500 towards freight and insurance, 15 bags are damaged in transit and the insurer pays therefore Rs. 1,000, to the consignor.

   B takes the delivery of the goods and immediately accepts a one month bill drawn on him for Rs. 20,000.

   The consignee thereafter reports:

   (i) the sale of 70 bags at Rs. 350 each;
   (ii) the sale of the damaged bags @ Rs. 110 each; and
   (iii) the incurrence of the (a) clearing charges Rs. 1,020, (b) godown rent Rs. 700 and carriage outwards Rs. 300.

   He is entitled to a commission @ 10% on the sale proceeds of all goods excepting damaged goods. Assuming that B remits the balance by a crossed bank draft, and no portion of the consignee's expenses is attributable to the damaged bags, show the important most ledger accounts in the books of A.

5. Mr. Achut to Mumbai consigned 100 units of a commodity to Mr. Rao of Delhi. The goods were invoiced at Rs. 150 so as to yield a profit of 50 per cent on cost. Mr Achut incurred Rs. 1,000 on freight and insurance. Mr. Rao incurred Rs. 500 on freight and Rs. 800 on rent. He sold 50 units for cash at Rs. 160 per unit, and 20 units at Rs. 175 on credit. He retained his commission of 6 per cent (including

del-credere) and remitted the balance. Mr. Rao noticed that 10 units were damaged on account of bad packing and were saleable only for Rs. 80 per unit. A debtor for Rs. 1,000 to whom the goods were sold by Mr. Rao became insolvent and only 50 paise in a rupee was recovered.

Make necessary ledger entries in the books of Mr. Achut and Mr. Rao.

6. On 1st September, 2007 Shri S. Gupta of Mumbai sent 500 cases @ Rs. 150 each to Shri Menon of Chennai to be sold on his account and at his risk for 7 ½ % commission and 2 ½ % del-credere commission, and incurred Rs. 5,500 expenses Rs. 20,000 advance has been received on 31st December 2007. Shri Menon sent an Account Sale disclosing that 300 cases have been sold for Rs. 230 each and another 100 cases @ Rs. 220 each. He has incurred unloading expenses etc. Rs. 750 and selling expenses Rs. 1,000. He sends a bank draft for the net amount due. Prepare (a) Account Sales and (b) Ledger Accounts in the books of Shri S. Gupta.

7. Ali of Calcutta sent a consignment of cotton goods to Osman of Delhi invoiced at Rs. 1,000. The invoice price was made by adding 25% to the cost. The expenses incurred by Ali were: Packing Rs. 24, Carriage etc. Rs. 16, Insurance Rs. 12 and other expenses Rs. 26.

After three months he received an Account Sales intimating that half the consignment was sold at Rs. 600. The expenses incurred by the consignee were : Freight Rs. 30, fire Insurance Rs. 18 and other expenses Rs. 10. His commission was 6% on sales and del-credere commission 1 ½ %.

But no sale could be made of the remainder, so that it was brought back after another nine months at a further cost of Rs. 60. The goods were damaged and valued at 20% below cost.

Give ledger accounts in the books of both parties.

[Delhi, B.Com. (Pass), 1986 & 1993, 2002 (modified)]

8. Arun sends goods on consignment to Seemu. The terms are that Seemu will receive 10% commission on the invoice price (which is cost plus 25%) and 20% of any price realized above the invoice price. Seemu will meet his expenses himself, goods to be sent freight paid. Arun sent goods whose cost was Rs. 16,000 and spent Rs. 1,500 on freight, forwarding etc. Seemu accepted a bill for Rs. 16,000 immediately on receiving the consignment. His expenses were Rs. 200 as rent and Rs. 100 as insurance. Seemu sold 3/4 of the goods for Rs. 19,500. Part of the sales were on credit and one customer failed to pay Rs. 400. Give consignment account and Seemu's account in the books of Arun and Arun's account in the books of Seemu.

9. X of Calcutta sent on 15th January, 2007, a consignment of 500 bicycles, costing Rs. 100 each, Expenses of Rs. 700 met by the consignor. Y of Mumbai spent Rs. 1,500 for clearance and the selling expenses were Rs. 10 per bicycle.

Y sold on 4th April, 2007, 300 bicycles @ Rs. 160 per bicycle and again on 20th June, 2007, 150 bicycles @ Rs. 172 each.

Y was entitled to a commission of Rs. 25 per bicycle sold plus one-fourth of the amount by which the gross sale proceeds less total commission there on exceeded a sum calculated at the rate of Rs. 125 per bicycle sold.

Y sent the amount due to X on 30th June, 2007.

You are required to show the Consignment Account and Y's Account in the books of X.

10. On 1st January, 2008, Badri of Mumbai consigned 100 cases (cost price Rs. 7,500) at pro-forma invoice price of 25% profit on sales to his agent Anil of Allahabad. On the same date Badri paid non-recurring expenses of Rs. 600. On 10th January, Anil took delivery and paid Rs. 1,200 for Octroi and other duties and remitted Rs. 4,000 as an advance against the consignment on 31st January. He sold 80 cases for Rs. 10,500. Anil is entitled to 5% commission on gross sales and 10% on the sale price in excess of invoice price.

Show Ledger Accounts in the books of Badri.

[Delhi, B.Com.(Pass), 1987, Correspondence Courses, 1995]

11. B of Mumbai consigns goods to C of Cochin to be sold at or above invoice price. C is to get 10% commission on sales at invoice price plus 20% of any surplus price realized. B draws on C at 60 days sight for 50% of invoice price the balance of proceeds being remitted by bank draft by C after deduction of his commission immediately upon sale.

During the year ended 31st March 2007, B consigned to C goods whose total cost including freight was Rs. 1,50,000 and the invoice price of which was Rs. 2,25,000. Sales by C during the year amounted to Rs. 2,05,000. On 31st March 2007, goods unsold with C were of invoice price of Rs. 67,500. During the year , B had received from C by bank draft Rs. 49,750 certain remittance being in transit on 31st March 2007.

Show the ledger accounts in the books of B recording the above transactions, closing the books of accounts on 31st March 2007.

12. Shri M. S. sent goods to Shri JP to be sold on consignment basis @5% commission. Goods costing Rs. 4,00,000 were sent and expenses of Rs. 40,000 were incurred. Shri JP had incurred Rs. 10,000 expenses for unloading and 75% of the goods were sold for Rs. 4,80,000. Shri JP sent the amount due from him with account sale, but wanted to return the remaining goods as he was not agreeable to carry on as a commission agent. He was however, to continue on Joint Venture basis for one-forth (1/4) profit Rs. 2,00,000 worth of goods was further despatched by Shri M.S. All the goods (except Rs. 20,000 which were taken over by Shri JP for the same amount) were sold for Rs. 5,00,000. Shri M.S. incurred Rs. 20,000 expenses and expenses of Shri JP amount to Rs. 17,000. Show the necessary accounts in the books of Shri M.S.

13. On 1st September, 2008, goods of the value of Rs. 66,000 were consigned by R. Brothers of Rewari to their agent B. Brothers of Mumbai at pro-forma invoice price of 20% profit on cost. R brothers paid forwarding charges and insurance amounting to Rs. 2,500. B. Brothers were allowed Rs. 3,000 per annum being the establishment cost, 6% commission on gross Sale, 3% del-credere commission after charging such commission B. Brothers made an expense of Rs. 700 as clearing charges. 3/4 of the goods were sold at 33 % profit on cost, half of which were credit sales and 1/2 of the balance goods were destroyed by fire and claim lodged for Rs. 8,000 was settled at a discount of 20%. Show consignment a/c, consignee a/c, Goods sent on consignment a/c and stock destroyed by fire a/c as on 31st December, 2008 in the books of R. Brothers of Rewari. Balance of stock was valued at pro-forma invoice price. [Delhi. B.Com. (Pass), 1998 (B)]

14. Deepak sold goods on behalf of Geep Sales Corporation on consignment basis. On 1st January, 2008 he had with him a stock of Rs. 20,000 on consignment. During the year he received goods worth Rs. 2,00,000.

Deepak had instruction to sell the goods at cost plus 25% and was entitled to a commission of 4% on sales, addition to 1% del-credere commission.

During the year ended 31st December, 2008, Cash sales were Rs. 1,20,000 and credit sales Rs. 1,05,000. Deepak expenses relating to consignment Rs. 3,000 being salaries and insurance and bad debts Rs. 3,000. From the above, prepare necessary accounts in the books of Geep Sales Corporation.

15. Star Mills Ltd., Surat sends regular consignment of yarn to X who is the selling agent of the Mill and is entitled to a commission of 10 paise per kg. of yarn sold. This included del-credere commission. Following further information is furnished to you:

On 1st July 2007, stock of yarn with the agent 20,000 kg costing Rs. 50,000. During the year ended 30th June, 2008. Total quantity of yarn consigned 1,60,000 kg. at Rs. 3 per kg.

Total quantity of yarn sold 1,50,000 kg. at Rs. 3.75 per kg.

These included the opening stock of 20,000 kg.

Total remittances by the Agent Rs. 5,10,000. Railway Freight paid by the agent Rs. 40,000 of the sales made, X could not collect Rs. 11,000 due to the insolvency of the customer.

5,000 kg of yarn were damaged in transit by Railway for which the agent recovered Rs. 6,000. The damaged goods were sold at the rate of Rs. 1.50 per kg.

Show the following ledger accounts in the books of Star Mills Ltd. For the year ended 30th June, 2008.

(a) Consignment a/c,

(b) X's a/c, and

(c) Goods Damaged in Transit a/c.

16. Nav Jagriti Sangam consigned goods to X of the cost of Rs. 5,000 and invoiced the same at pro-forma invoice price at 20% above cost. The consignor paid Rs. 120 for freight etc. and received a bill from Y on account for Rs. 2,000 and discounted it for Rs. 1,950.

X sold 3/4 goods for cash and credit for Rs. 5,200. One customer failed to pay Rs.200 due to his insolvency. X paid Rs. 80 for loading and unloading and Rs. 255 for rent etc. The consignee was entitled to a commission $7\frac{1}{2}$ % on sales. Account was settled by cheque.

Prepare necessary accounts in the books of the consignor. [Delhi, B.Com.(Pass), 1990 (Supple)]

17. X sent goods to Y to be sold on consignment basis. The invoice price was Rs. 24,000 which was 20% above cash. Y was entitled to a commission of 5% on the invoice price of the goods sold and 15% on any excess price realized. On receiving the goods Y paid Rs. 920 as freight and Rs. 500 as rent etc. He sold 5/8 of the goods for Rs. 19,000. Part of the sales was on credit and there was a bad debt of Rs. 600. Y settled his account by cheque.

Show necessary accounts in the books of X.

[Delhi, B.Com. (Pass), 1990 (B)]

18. Nagaraj of Calcutta consigned 100 radio sets costing Rs. 500 each to Ramlal of Patna. The invoice was made pro-forma at Rs. 600 per set. Ram Lal was entitled to a commission of $7\frac{1}{2}$ % on sales plus $2\frac{1}{2}$ % del-credere commission and 10% of any excess price realized over invoice price. Ram Lal was to bear all expenses incurred after the goods reached his godown. While sending the goods, Nagaraj paid Rs. 1,500 as forwarding expenses and insurance. In transit, 10 radio sets were damaged and Nagaraj recovered Rs. 4,000 from Insurance Company. Ram Lal took delivery of the remaining radio sets paying Rs. 4,500 as freight, cartage etc. Ram Lal sold 70 radio sets at Rs. 800 each, 30 of them on credit. Out of which the proceeds of 3 radio sets could not be recovered because of disappearance of the customers. He paid Rs. 500 as storage and selling expenses. Ram Lal sent a Bank draft for the amount due to Nagaraj.

Show consignment account, Ram Lal's Account, Goods destroyed A/c and Goods sent on consignment a/c in the books of Nagaraj.

[Delhi, B.Com. (Pass) 2000]

19. M of Bangalore sent goods to B of Kolkata to be sold on behalf of M. B getting a commission (including del-credere commission) of 10% on sales effected by him. All expenses were to be borne by M. The invoice value of goods was Rs. 3,00,000 made up as cost plus 20%. M spent Rs. 5,000 on forwarding and packing. B paid the following:

Particulars	*Rs.*
Freight and cartage to godown	16,000
Storage	3,000
Insurance	2,000
Miscellaneous	1,000

At the end of 3 months B reported that he had sold 3/5 of the goods for Rs. 2,00,000. He returned 1/5 of the goods to M as unsalable in Calcutta but he was confident of selling the remaining goods. M paid Rs. 3,500 as freight on the returned goods. One customer, who had bought on credit failed to pay Rs. 8,000 due from him.

Ascertain, by preparing relevant accounts, the profit or loss suffered by the two parties.

[Delhi, B.Com (Pass) 2001]

20. Punjab Cycle Co. of Ludhiana consigned 100 bicycles to Kanpur Cycle Co. of Kanpur costing Rs. 1,500 each, invoiced at Rs. 2,000 each. The Consignor paid freight Rs. 10,000 and insurance in transit Rs. 1,500. During transit, 10 bicycles were totally damaged. Kanpur Cycle co. took delivery of the remaining bicycles and paid Rs. 1,530 for octroi duty. Kanpur Cycle Co. sent a bank draft to Punjab cycle co. for Rs. 50,000 as advance and later on sent an account sales showing that 80 bicycles had been sold @ Rs. 2,200 each. Expenses incurred by Kanpur Cycle Co. on godown rent were Rs. 2,000. Kanpur Cycle Co. is entitled to a commission of 5% on invoice price and 25% on any surplus of sale price over invoice price. Insurance claim was settled at Rs. 14,000.

Prepare consignment account, consignee's account and accidental loss account in the books of the Consignor.

(C.S. Foundation, Dec., 1996)

21. X of Kolkata, on 15th January, 2007 sent to Y of Mumbai a consignment of 250 televisions costing Rs. 10,000 each. Expenses of Rs. 7,000 were met by the Consignor. Y of Mumbai spent Rs. 4,500 for clearance on 30th January, 1997 and the selling expenses were Rs. 500 per television sold as and when the sales made by Y.

Y sold on 4th March, 2007, 150 televisions @ Rs. 14,000 per television and again on 10th April, 2007, 75 televisions at Rs. 14,400 each.

Mr. Y was entitled to a commission of Rs. 500 per television sold plus one-fourth of the amount by which the gross sale proceeds less total commission thereon exceeding a sum calculated at the rate of Rs. 12,500 per television sold. Y sent the amount sale and the amount due to X on 30th April 2007 by bank draft.

You are required to show the Consignment account and Y's account in the books of X.

(C.A. Foundation, May 1997)

22. Ashish of Delhi sent on consignment 500 boxes to Nishank of Mumbai at an invoice price of Rs. 150 each which is cost plus 25%. Ashish spent Rs. 2,000 on freight and Rs. 500 on insurance. Ashish received a draft of Rs. 20,000 from Nishank as advance. Nishank received 450 boxes (50 boxes were lost in transit). Nishank spent Rs. 1,000 on carriage, Rs. 350 on octroi and Rs. 2,000 as Salesmen's commission. Nishank is entitled to a commission of 10% on gross sales, 2% del-credere commission on credit sales and 20% on any surplus realized over invoice price. Nishank sold 200 boxes on cash basis at Rs. 170 each and 225 boxes on credit at Rs. 200 each. One customer who was sold 20 boxes on credit became insolvent and only 50 paise in a rupee could be realized from his estate. Insurance company admitted a claim Rs. 7,200 for the goods lost in transit.

Prepare Consignment Account, Loss in Transit Account and Nishank's Account in the books of Ashish.

ANSWERS

B. Objective type questions.

1. (a) III (b) III (c) III (d) II (e) II
2. I (False) II False III False IV True V False VI False VII False

C. Exercises

			Rs.
1.	I	Profit on consignment	9,320
	II	Value of unsold stock	15,700
	III	Balance of Prashant's a/c	58,200
2	(a)	Profit on consignment	781
	(b)	Value of unsold stock	15,684.50
	(c)	Abnormal Loss	5,684.50
	(d)	B's a/c - Balance payable	32,150
3.	(i)	Profit on Consignment	1,975
	(ii)	Value of unsold stock	2,100
	(iii)	Amount remitted by G. Prasad	20,875
4.	(i)	Loss on consignment a/c	1,170
	(ii)	Consignee's a/c	26,150

	(iii)	Bank cover draft	1,680
5.	(i)	Profit on consignment a/c	1,960
	(ii)	Cash payable to Mr. Achut	9,510
	(iii)	Total of Delhi consignment a/c	20,950
	(iv)	Commission	190
6.	(i)	Profit on consignment	15,900
	(ii)	Balance payable	60,150
	(iii)	Value of unsold stock	16,250
7.	(i)	Loss on consignment	121
	(ii)	Commission payable	45
	(iii)	Value of unsold stock	320
8.	(i)	Profit on consignment	3,575
	(ii)	Commission payable to Seemu (1500+900)	2,400
	(iii)	Amount due from Seemu	700
9.	(i)	Profit on consignment	9,810
	(ii)	Commission payable	12,510
	(iii)	Balance payable by YHint = Let total commission be XX = No. of bicycles sold X 25 + ¼ [Gross Sale proceeds No. of bicycles sold x 125-X]= 450 x 25+ ¼ [73,800-450 125 -X]= 11,250+ ¼ [17,550 - X] 4X = 45,000 + 17,550 - X5X = 62,550 or X = Rs. 12,510	55,290
10.	(i)	Profit on consignment	2,285
	(ii)	Value of unsold stock	2,360
	(iii)	Commission payable Rs. 525+250	775
11.	(i)	Profit on consignment	70,000
	(ii)	Commission	30,000
12.	(i)	Profit on consignment	1,18,500
	(ii)	Profit on Joint Venture	1,70,500
	(iii)	Value of unsold stock	1,12,500
	(iv)	Commission payable	24,000
13.	(i)	Profit on consignment	7,409
	(ii)	Abnormal Loss	3,900
14.	(i)	Profit on consignment	40,875
	(ii)	Value of unsold stock	40,000
	(iii)	Amount payable	2,20,875
15.	(i)	Profit on consignment	75,000
	(ii)	Value of unsold stock	81,250
	(iii)	X's balance outstanding	10,500
	(iv)	Abnormal Loss	3,250
16.	(i)	Profit on consignment	405
	(ii)	Value of unsold stock	1,550
	(iii)	X's A/c	2,275
17.	(i)	Profit on consignment	3,475
	(ii)	Value of unsold stock	9,345

	(iii)	Commission payable to X	1,350
	(iv)	Consignment a/c	55,290
18.	(i)	Profit on consignment	9,450
	(ii)	Value of unsold stock	13,300
	(iii)	Commission payable 5,600 + 1,400	7,000
	(iv)	X's account (Balance payable)	44,500
19.	(i)	Profit on Consignment	3,700
	(ii)	Value of unsold stock	64,200
	(iii)	Commission Payable	20,000
20.	(i)	Profit on consignment	31,440
	(ii)	Value of unsold stock	21,320
	(iii)	Abnormal Loss	16,150
	(iv)	Commission	12,000
21.	(i)	Profit on consignment	6,43,750
	(ii)	Value of unsold stock	2,51,150
	(iii)	Commission	1,63,500
22.	(i)	Profit on consignment	10,750
	(ii)	Value of unsold stock	3,950
	(iii)	Loss in transit (Abnormal Loss)	6,250
	(iv)	Commission	11,850
	(v)	Balance of Sunil's A/c	43,800

CHAPTER 16

JOINT VENTURE ACCOUNTS

A. Essay Type Questions

1. What is Joint Venture? Explain its advantages.
2. Distinguish between
   (a) Joint Venture and Partnership. [Delhi, B.Com.(Pass) 1992, 2005]
   (b) Joint Venture and Consignment. [Delhi. B.Com (Pass),1998]
3. Explain the meaning of Joint venture, State the accounts which are opened for a joint venture under Separate set of books method. [Delhi, B.Com (Pass), 1996]

B. Objective Type Questions

1. State whether the following statements are true or false.
   (i) A Co-venturer is an agent of another venturer.
   (ii) Joint venture and partnership are synonymous.
   (iii) Life of the joint Venture is limited.
   (iv) Each venturer gets commission.
   (v) Joint venture can be converted into consignment at any time.
2. Put a correct answer –
   (i) Joint venture is a
      (a) Personal account
      (b) Real Account
      (c) Nominal account.
   (ii) When goods are purchased for the joint venture, the account debited is
      (i) Purchases account
      (ii) Venturer a/c
      (iii) Joint Venture Account.
   (iii) When goods are sold which account is credited
      (i) Venturer a/c
      (ii) Sales a/c
      (iii) Joint venture account.
   (iv) Joint Bank a/c is opened when
      (I) Each venturer keeps the books
      (II) All venturers keep the books
      (III) Separate set of books are maintained.

C. Exercises

1. Rakesh and Mukesh agree to enter into a Joint Venture. They agree to share the profits and losses in the ratio 3: 1, Rakesh supplied goods worth Rs. 5,000 and incurred an expenditure of Rs. 600 on Joint Venture. Mukesh supplied goods worth Rs. 8,000 and spent Rs. 800. Mukesh sold the goods on behalf of the Joint Venture for Rs. 18,000. He is also entitled to receive a commission @ 2 □ %. He remitted the balance to Rakesh as per Bank draft.

   Open the necessary ledger accounts in the books of both the parties.

2. A and B enter into a joint venture. They agree to share profits and losses as to A 75% and to B 25%. A sends Rs. 50,000 to B. The latter purchases several varieties of silk goods and sends them to A. The particulars of such purchases are given below:

   1,000 ladies garments @ Rs. 10 each, 2,000 silk shirts @ Rs. 15 each, 500 silk pujamies @ Rs. 20 each. The expenses incurred by B amounted to Rs. 500. A sells the first two varieties at double the price but in respect of pujamies he made a profit of Rs. 5,000 only. His expenses amounted to Rs. 2,000.

   Prepare necessary accounts in the books of A.

3. Das and Krishan entered into a joint venture sharing profits and losses as 3:2. They opened a Bank a/c by depositing Rs. 40,000 each.

   Das purchased 800 kg. Of an item @ Rs. 60 and his expenses were Rs. 13,000. Krishan purchased a second item of 10,000 kg. @ Rs. 2.10 and his expenses were Rs. 11,000. Expenses were met in private sources and purchases were paid for from bank a/c.

   Krishan sold 600 kg. of the first item @ Rs. 100/kg and his selling expenses were Rs. 5,500. Das sold 8,000 kg. of the second item @ Rs. 5.00/kg. and his selling expenses were Rs. 6,000. All the sale proceeds were deposited in a Bank a/c and expenses were met from private sources.

   Write up necessary accounts in the books of the venture. Also prepare a Balance Sheet of the venture.

4. A trader, X agrees to sell a pearl necklace, which costs Rs. 15,000, on behalf of Y on the term that the net profit on the transaction was to be shared equally between them, interest being calculated @ 5% on the date of agreement, X gives Y a six month's bill of exchange for Rs. 7,500, and four months later he sells the necklace for Rs. 18,000 for cash. On the date of sale, he settles with Y. How much should he pay? Prepare Joint Venture a/c.

5. Ramesh of Allahabad and Suresh of Banaras enter into a Joint Venture to consign 100 bags of sugar to Mahesh of Patna, to be sold on their joint risk which is in the ratio of 3/5 and 2/5 respectively.

   Ramesh sends 60 bags of sugar at Rs. 1,300 each paying for freight and other charges amounting to Rs. 900. Suresh sends 40 bags of sugar at Rs. 1,250 each paying for freight and other charges amounting to Rs. 800. All the bags of sugar are sold by the consignee for Rs. 1,50,000. Out of which he deducts Rs. 1,600 for his expenses and his commission at 3%. He remits a bank draft of Rs. 70,000 to Ramesh and another to Suresh for the balance.

   Prepare Joint Venture a/c and Suresh a/c in the books of Ramesh and Ramesh's a/c in the books of Suresh.

6. A and B enter into joint venture and purchase an old house for Rs. 5,000 each contributing Rs. 2,500, for an agreed fee of Rs. 200. A is to arrange the disposal of the property sale of interior's windows etc., amount to Rs. 1,500. A pays Rs. 200 for demolishing the house, the material of which realize Rs. 190, Sundry charges paid were Rs. 80 and the whole of the land is sold for Rs. 7,000. A and B share the net profits equally. A paying B his share in cheque. You are required to journalise the entries and Prepare Joint Venture a/c and B's a/c in the ledger of A.

7. Anand and Pramod entered into a speculative venture of underwriting the subscription at par of the entire share capital of the Rajasthan Mines Ltd., consisting of 10,000 equity shares of Rs. 10 each and to pay all expenses upto allotment. The profits were to be shared to them in proportion of 3/5 and 2/5. The consideration in return for this guarantee was 1,200 equity shares of Rs. 10 each fully paid to be issued to them.

   Anand provided funds for Registration fees Rs. 1,200, advertising Rs. 1,100, Printing and distributing prospectus Rs. 750 and other Printing and Stationary Rs. 200. Pramod contributed towards payment of office rent Rs. 300, legal expenses Rs. 1,375, clerical staff Rs. 900 and other disbursements Rs. 175. The prospectus was issued and the applications from the public fell short of the full issue by 1,500 shares. Anand purchased these shares on joint account and the same in full.

   They received 1,200 fully paid equity shares as underwriting commission. Anand and Pramod sold their entire holdings at Rs. 12.50 less Rs. 0.50 per share for brokerage. The net proceeds were received by Anand for 1,500 shares and Pramod for 1,200 shares.

Write up the necessary accounts in the books of both the parties showing the final adjustment.

[Delhi, B.Com. (Pass), 1998]

8. Joseph and David entered into a Joint Venture for purchasing the goods at an auction and selling the same at a profit. The profits and losses were to be shared by them in the ratio of 2:1. Joseph purchased goods for Rs. 2,40,000 for cash.

He drew a bill of exchange of David for Rs. 90,000 for three months duration. Joseph got this bill discounted from his bank at a discount of 12% per annum. The following transactions took place during the course of the venture.

(i) Joseph spent Rs. 3,600 for conveyance, Rs. 4,800 for salary and Rs. 300 for traveling expenses.

(ii) David spent Rs. 1,500 for traveling expenses and Rs. 900 for miscellaneous expenses.

(iii) Joseph sold part of the goods for Rs. 2,25,000 and David for Rs. 1,80,000.

(iv) Goods costing Rs. 9,000 and Rs. 6,000 were taken up by David and Joseph respectively at 20% above the cost.

(v) David was to be allowed Rs. 2,400 for his godown having been used for joint venture purposes.

(vi) Joseph was allowed a salary of Rs. 6,000 per month for three months.

(vii) Discount on bill of exchange was to be treated as the expense of the joint venture. Assuming that no separate set of books of accounts are maintained for the joint venture and the accounts are settled. Prepare Joint Venture a/c with David and David a/c in the books of Joseph.

9. Ramlal and Shyamlal entered into a joint venture for purchase and sale of cotton. They agreed to share profits in the proportion of 2:1 and also to be entitled to an interest of 6% per annum (on monthly basis) on capital invested by each of them. The following transactions took place in between themselves:

(i) On 1st Nov. 2006, Ramlal purchased 700 bales of cotton @ Rs. 110 per bale, the brokerage being Rs. 4 per bale.

(ii) On 1st Dec., 2006, Shyamlal purchased 600 bales of cotton @ Rs. 124 per bale, the brokerage being Rs. 4 per bale.

(iii) On 1st Jan., 2007, Shyamlal sold 350 bales of cotton @ Rs. 138 per bale (the brokerage being Rs. 2 per bale) and took the proceeds to himself.

(iv) On 15th January, 2007, Ramlal sold 800 bales of cotton @ Rs. 132 per bale (the brokerage being Rs. 2 per bale) and took the sale proceeds to himself.

It was also agreed that each of the partners will at first sell from his own purchase and then if required, from the stock purchased by the other one. The balance of stock was to be divided between the partners in proportion of their profit sharing ratio, goods being valued at cost to the partner concerned.

On 31st Jan, 2007, the partners settled their accounts. Show the Accounts of Ramlal and Shyamlal and the joint venture as would appear when maintained in a separate set of books.

10. Gavaskar and Biswanath jointly underwrite and place on the market 50,000 shares of Bombay Machineries Ltd. of Rs. 10 each. It was agreed with the company that they would be allotted 2,000 shares as fully paid towards their remuneration. Their profit sharing ratio is 3:2.

Applications are received from the public only for 45,000 shares. Gavaskar paid Rs. 4,000 for postage and advertisement in addition to 60% of the amount required to take up the short subscription.

Biswanath financed the balance amount. These are accounted for through joint Bank Account. All the shares including those allotted for remuneration were sold. Gavaskar sold 3000 shares for Rs. 35,000 and Biswanath sold the balance shares for Rs. 48000. Biswanath incurred expenses Rs. 2,000. Sale proceeds were retained individually.

Show necessary accounts in the books of the venturers which were separately started for this purpose. Was settled through the Bank Account.

[Delhi, B. Com. (Pass) 2001 (B)]

11. A and B enter into a joint Venture to prepare a film for the government. The Government agrees to pay Rs. 1,00,000. A contributes Rs. 10,000 and B contributes Rs. 15,000. These amounts are paid into a joint Bank Account. Payments made out of the joint Account were:

	Rs.
Purchase of Equipment	6,000
Hire of Equipment	5,000
Wages	45,000
Materials	10,000
Office Expenses	5,000

A paid Rs. 2,000 as Licensing Fees. On completion, the film was found defective and Government made a deduction of Rs. 10,000. The equipment was taken over by B at a valuation of Rs. 2,000.

Separate books were maintained for the joint Venture where profits were divided in the ratio of 2:3. Give the necessary ledger accounts.

[Delhi, B.Com. (Pass) , 1993, (B)]

12. A of Agra and B of Mumbai enter into a Joint Venture to consign 200 bales of cloth to D of Delhi to be sold on their joint risk which is in the proportion of 3/7 and 4/7 respectively. A sends 150 bales at Rs. 2600 each, paying for freight and other charges Rs. 4900. B sends 50 bales at Rs. 2500 each, paying for expenses Rs. 3600. All the bales were sold by D for Rs. 14,00,000 of which D deducts Rs. 6,000 for his expenses and 10% on total sales as his commission. D remits Rs. 3,00,000 to A and Balance amount to B through Bank draft.

Prepare necessary ledger accounts in the books of both coventurers.

[Delhi, B.Com (Pass) 1997]

13. D and R doing business separately as building contractors. They under took jointly to construct a new building for a company for a contract price of Rs. 1340000, Rs. 840000 to be paid in cash and balance in fully paid shares of the company.

A joint bank account was opened towards which D contributed Rs. 4,50,000 and R Rs. 2,00,000. The profit and loss is to shared in the ratio of 3:2

The Transactions were as follows:

Particulars	Rs.
Amount Advanced to suppliers for supply of Materials	5,20,000
Value of Materials supplied by the suppliers	8,90,000
Wages paid	3,60,000
Materials Purchased for Cash	25,000
Materials supplied by D	92,500
Architecture Fees paid	32,500
Value of stock lost by fire not recovered by insurance	35,500
Balance amount paid to suppliers	

The contract was completed and the contract price was duly received. D took all the shares for Rs. 4,70,000 and R took the balance of stock of Materials worth Rs. 35,000 at an agreed value of Rs. 27,500.

Prepare necessary ledger accounts.

[Delhi, B.Com (pass) 1999 (b)]

14. Ram and Mohan entered into a joint venture to purchase and sell new year gifts and to share profits and losses equally.

On 4th November 2007 Ram purchased goods costing Rs. 1,00,000 and spent Rs. 6,000 for sending them to Mohan and also paid Rs. 2000 for insurance. On the same date Ram drew a Bill for Rs. 100000 on Mohan for two months. The bill was accepted by Mohan and Ram discounted the same @ 18% p.a.

Mohan paid Rs. 3,000 for cartage, Rs. 5000 for rent and Rs. 5,000 for advertisement. He sold all the gifts for Rs. 2,00,000 after retaining gifts worth Rs. 2,000 for his personal use. On 8th January 2008 Mohan sent a cheque for the amount due to Ram. You are required to prepare (1) memorandum Joint Venture Account; (2) Joint Venture with Mohan Account in the books of Ram.

(C.S. Foundation, June 1998)

15. Dilip and Dev enter into a joint venture to import cloth. On 1st January, 2006 they opened joint bank account with Canara Bank, Dilip contributing Rs 2,00,000 and Dev Rs. 1,00,000. They agreed to share profits in the ratio of the capital introduced by them. On 15th February, 2006 they remitted to a manufacturer in U.K. Rs 2,50,000 for goods received and incurred expenses of Rs 8,000 for freight insurance etc. The goods were sold for Rs. 3,30,000 for which the selling expenses were as follows:

    Godown rent Rs. 2,000, Commission payable to Dev on the gross amount of sales 10%, Miscellaneous expenses amounted to Rs. 3,000.

    Prepare necessary ledger accounts.

16. Aashu and Ish entered into joint venture to construct a cinema half for a price of Rs.3,00,000 for this purpose Aashu put Rs. 60,000 and Ish Rs. 50,000 into a joint Bank Account opened for this purpose. The payments amounted to as follows:

Materials	Rs. 37,500
Wages	Rs. 60,000
Plant	Rs. 7,500

    These payments were made from Joint Bank Account but in addition, Aashu supplied cement bags valued at Rs. 7,500. The cinema hall was constructed but due to certain defects, the owner deducted Rs. 60,000 from the payment, which was made gradually. The plant was taken over by Ish at Rs. 4,000 and unused cement was taken back by Aashu at Rs. 2,000. They shared the profits in the ratio of 2:1. Show necessary ledger accounts.

    (Delhi, B.Com. (Pass) 1996)

17. X and Y enter into a joint venture and agree to share profit and losses in proportion of 4: 1 respectively. X supplies goods of the value of Rs. 10,000 and incurs expenses amounting ot Rs. 800. Y supplies goods of the value of Rs. 8,000 and his expenses amount to Rs. 600. Y sells goods on behalf of the joint venture and realizes Rs. 24,000.

    Y is entitled to a commission of 5% on sales.

    Y settles his account by bank draft.

    Give the journal entries and the relevant ledger accounts in the books of X.

ANSWER

A. Objective type questions

(1) (i) False (ii) false (iii) True (iv) false (v) true

(2) (i) c (ii) III (iii) III (iv) III

C. Exercise

	Rs.
1. Profit on Joint Venture	3,150
2. (i) Profit on joint Venture to A	31,875
To B	10,625
(ii) A remits to B	11,125
3. (i) Profit on Joint Venture Das	10,290
Krishan	6,860
(ii) Value of unsold stock Rs. 15250 + 6400	21,650
(iii) Total of Balance Sheet	1,32,650
4. (i) Profit on Joint Venture	2,750
(ii) Amount payable Rs. 7750 (Rs. 250 for interest) + 1375	
	9,125
5. (1) Profit on Joint Venture	14,200
(2) Suresh a/c balance	(+)17,420
(3) Ramesh's a/c balance	(–)17,420
6. Profit on Joint Venture	3,210
7. (1) Profit on Joint Venture	11,400
(Rs. 6840 + 4560)	
(2) Balance of Anand's A/c	19,090
(3) Balance of Pramod a/c	13,310
8. (1) Profit on Joint Venture a/c	1,48,800
(2) Balance of David's A/c payable	46,400
9. (1) Profit on Joint Venture	12,733
(2) Ram Lal pays shyamlal	27,574
(3) Interest credited to Ramlal	937
Shyamlal	530
10. (1) Net Profit Gavaskar	16,200
Biswanath	10,800
11. (i) Profit on Joint Venture	19,000
(ii) Amount payable to A	19,600
(iii) Amount payable to B	24,400
12. (i) Profit on Joint venture	7,30,500
(ii) Balance paid by D	9,54,000
13. (i) Loss on Joint Venture	62,000
D 37200	
R 24800	
(ii) Joint Bank Account (Total)	14,90,000
(iii) Balance Payable to D	34,800
R	1,47,700
14. (i) Profit on Joint Venture	78,000
(ii) Amount payable by Mohan	1,48,000
(iii) Amount receivable by Ram	1,50,000
(iv) Already received in the form of gift item	2,000

Contd...

15. (1) Profit on Joint Venture	34,000
(2) Dilip is paid	2,22,670
(3) Dev is paid	1,44,330
16. (i) Profit from Joint venture	1,33,500
(ii) Aashu receives	1,54,500
(iii) Ish receives	20,500
17. (i) Profit on Joint Venture	3,400
(ii) Amount received from Y	13,520

CHAPTER 17

BRANCH ACCOUNTS

A. Essay Type Questions

1. What are branch accounts? Distinguish between branch accounts and departmental accounts.
2. How many types of branches are there? What entries are made in the books of company to incorporate branch's trial balance?
3. Explain the causes of difference in the balances shown by the H.O. and the Branch.
4. How is normal and abnormal losses are treated in the branch account?
5. Explain the following:
   (a) Abnormal Loss [Delhi, B. Com (Pass) 2006 (B)]
   (b) Cash / Goods in Transit.
   (c) Loss of Goods in Transit.

B. Objective type Questions

1. Choose the Correct answers from the following
   (i) Branch account is under debtors system.
   (a) Personal a/c (b) Real A/c (c) Nominal A/c
   (ii) Under Independent branch, Branch account is a
   (a) Personal a/c (b) Real a/c (c) Nominal a/c
   (iii) Goods sent by the H.O. to the branch but not received by the branch are termed as -
   (a) Branch account (b) Goods in Transit a/c (c) None of the above.
   (iv) If % of profit on cost is 25% then how much % of profit on sales will be
   (i) 25% (ii) 20% (iii) 30%
   (v) If % of profit on sales in 25% then how much of profit on cost will be
   (i) 25% (ii) 20% (iii) $33\frac{1}{3}\%$
2. State whether the following statements are true or false.
   1. Branch a/c under a debtors system is a personal a/c.
   2. Branch a/c under independent branch is a personal a/c.
   3. Goods sent by the H.O. is not received by the branch, it is debited to goods in transit a/c.
   4. If% of profit on cost is 25% then it is 20% on sales.
   5. If % of profit on sales is 25% then it is 20% on costs.

C. Exercises

1. India Traders, Mumbai opened a branch at Baroda on 1st January 2006. The following information is available in respect of the branch for the year 2006.

	Rs.
Goods sent to the branch	75,000
Cash sales at the branch	50,000
Credit sales at the branch	60,000
Salaries o f the branch paid by the Head Office	15,000

Office Expenses of the branch paid by the Head Office	12,000
Cash remittances to branch towards petty cash	6,000
Petty cash at branch on 31.12.2006	500
Debtors at branch as on 31.12.2006	5,000
Stock at branch on 31.12.2006	27,000

Prepare Branch Account to show the profit/loss from the branch for the year 2006

2. A Head Office at Mumbai has branch at Chennai in charge of a manager. The ratio of gross profit on turnover at the branch was 25% constant throughout the year.

   The Branch manager is entitled to a commission of 10% of the profit earned by the branch calculated before charging his commission, but subject to a deduction from such commission a sum equal to 50% of any ascertained deficiency of Branch Stock. All goods were supplied to the branch by the Head Office.

   From the following figures extracted from the branch books, calculate the commission due to the manager for the year ended 31st December. 2006

Particulars	Rs.	Particulars	Rs.
Stock on 1.1.06 at Cost	31,210	Establishment Expenses	22,550
Goods received from Head Office at Cost	1,08,700	Drawings by Manager against Commission	1,000
Sales	1,46,400	Stock on 31.12.06 at Selling Price	39,880

3. From the following details prepare Branch Account in the books of Head Office:

	Rs.
Goods sent to branch at cost	50,000
Goods returned by branch at cost	3,000
Branch credit sales	51,000
Cash sales at branch	2,500
Cash remitted to head office by branch	45,000
Expenses paid \by head office	10,000
Discount allowed to customers by branch	1,800
Closing Stock with Branch at Cost	17,000
Branch Debtors (Closing balance)	7,700

4. Modi Brothers has branch at Lucknow, Goods are invoiced to his branch at 20% profit on invoice price. From the following details, prepare 'Branch Account' in the books of Head Office showing branch profit:

	Rs.
Credit sales	1,12,000
Goods supplied to branch at invoice price	3,80,000
Cash sales	2,48,000
Cash received from debtors	1,00,000
Wages (Paid by head office)	15,200
Rent (Paid by head office)	18,000
Discount allowed to customers	4,000
Sundry expenses (Paid by head office)	1,000
Goods returned by customers	2,000
Depreciation on furniture	1,000
Goods spoiled	1,000

5. X Ltd., Mumbai, started on 1st January 2006 has two branches at Kanpur and Lucknow. All goods sold at the branches are received from the Head Office invoiced at cost plus 25 per cent. All expenses relating to branches are paid by the head office. Each branch has its own sales ledger and sends weekly statement. All cash collections are remitted daily to head office by the branches. The following particulars relating to the year ended 31st December. 2006 have been extracted from the weekly statements sent by the branches:

Particulars	Kanpur (Rs.)	Lucknow (Rs.)
Credit Sales	1,25,200	1,10,000
Cash Sales	78,600	85,200
Sales Returns	2,300	1,200
Sundry Debtors	34,500	23,600
Rent and Rates	3,200	4,500
Bad debts	6,000	—
Salaries	1,6000	18,000
General Expenses	2,600	1,500
Goods received form Head Office	1,50,000	1,25,000
Advertisement	7,500	5,200
Stock on 31st December 2006	45,000	35,000

You are required to prepare Branch Accounts as they would appear in the books of the head office, showing the profit or loss for the period and Trading and Profit & Loss a/c separately for each branch.

6. X Co. Ltd. opened a branch at Jaipur on 1.1.06 The goods are sent by head office to the branch at invoice price which is 25% above cost price.

The following are the particulars relating to the transactions of Jaipur Branch:

	Rs.
Goods sent to Branch (at cost to head office)	2,80,800
Sales: Cash	1,25,000
Credit	1,75,000
Cash collected from Debtors	1,56,000.
Discount allowed	4,000
Cash sent to branch for	
Wages	5,000
Freight	11,000
Other Expenses	6,000
Spoiled cloth in bales written off at invoice price	500
Stock (at invoice price 31.12.06)	55,500

Ascertain the net profit made by the branch following Branch stock and Debtors system.

7. A Head Office in Mumbai has a branch in Delhi to which goods are invoiced by the Head Office at cost plus 20%. Prepare Branch Account in the books of Head Office from the following particulars:

	Rs.
Stock in the beginning	12,500
Debtors in the beginning	12,000
Goods received from Mumbai	40,000
Cash sales	16,000
Cash received from debtors	29,500
Goods returned to head office	2,000
Cash received for expenses	14,500
Stock at the end	15,000
Debtors at the end	22,500

[Delhi B.Com. (P) 1994 (Figures 5 times)]

8. X Ltd. operates a retail branch at Kanpur. All purchases are made by the head office in Calcutta, goods being charged out to the Branch at selling price which is cost plus 25%. All the expenses of branch are paid through head office cheques. Cash collected from customers as also the ready money sales are daily banked to the credit of the head office. From the following particulars of the branch write up the necessary accounts to arrive at the branch profit or loss in the head office books by using stock and debtors system:

Particulars	Rs.	Particulars	Rs.
Debtors at start	20,000	Invoiced Inventory at beginning	32,000
Debtors at end	24,000	Invoiced Inventory at end	30,000
Ready money sales during the year	1,40,000	Salaries	12,000
Cash Received on Ledger Account	1,30,000	Rent etc.	10,000
Return to H.O. at Invoiced Amount	5,000	Bad debts	4,000
Normal Leakage and Spoilage	4,000	Discount and Allowances	6,000

9. Messers Eastern Traders, Deihi, have opened a branch at Jaipur on 1.7.2006. The goods were sent by the Head Office to the branch and invoiced at selling price which was 125% of the cost price of the H.O.

The following are the particulars relating to the transactions of Jaipur Branch:

Particulars	Rs.	Particulars	Rs.
Goods Sent to Branch (at cost to H.O)	2,80,800	Discount Allowed	4,000
Sales : Cash	1,25,000	Stock on June 30, 2007 at Invoice Price	55,500
Credit	1,75,000	Cash Sent to Branch for Wages	3,000
Cash Collected from Debtors	1,56,000	Freight	11,000
		Other Expenses	6,000

Spoiled cloth in bales written off at invoice price Rs. 500.

Prepare Branch Debtors, Branch Stock, Branch Adjustment and Branch P & L account s in H.O. Books.

[Delhi, B. Com. (Hons.), 1994]

10. Shri X has a branch in Calcutta. He invoices goods to the branch at selling price which is cost plus $33\frac{1}{3}\%$. From the following particulars, prepare Branch Account and Goods sent to branch account in the books of Shri X :

Particulars		Rs.	Particulars		Rs.
Stock on 1st Jan., 06 (Invoice price)		15,000	Cash received from Debtors		40,000
Debtors on 1st Jan. 06		11,400	Discount allowed to Customers		300
Goods invoiced to Branch during the			Bad debts written off		250
year at invoice price		67,000	Cheques sent to Branch:		
Sales at Branch:			Salaries	5,000	
Cash	Rs. 31000		Sundry Expenses	1,700	6,700
Credit	Rs. 37400	68400	Stock on 31st Dec. 06 (Invoice price)		13,400

11. X Ltd., operates a retail a retail branch at Nasik. All purchases are made by the head office in Calcutta goods being charged out to the branch at selling price which is cost plus 25%. All the expenses of branch are paid through head office cheques, cash collected from customers as also the ready money sales are daily banked to the credit of the head office. From the following particulars of the branch write up the necessary accounts to arrive at the branch profit or loss in the head office books by using stock and debtors system:

Particulars	Rs.	Particulars	Rs.
Debtors at start	10,000	Invoice inventory at end	15,000
Debtors at end	12,000	Salaries	6,000
Ready money sales during the year	70,000	Rent etc.	5,000
Cash received on ledger account	65,000	Bad debts	2,000
Returns to H.O. at invoiced amount	5,000	Discount & Allowances	3,000
Invoice inventory at beginning	16,000	Normal leakage and spoilage	4,000

12. P. Ltd invoiced goods to its A branch @ 20% less than the catalogue price which is cost plus 50% with instructions that cash sales were to be made at invoice price and credit sales at catalogue price less discount at 15% on prompt payment. From the following details, prepare the Branch Trading and Profit & Loss account for the year ended 31st Dec., in the head office books so as to show the true result of the branch operations for the year.

Particulars	Rs.	Particulars	Rs.
Invoiced Stock Jan. 1	12,000	Salaries rent etc. (paid by head office)	13,650
Dec. 31	15,000	Cash Received from Debtors	85,635
Debtors Jan. 1	10,000	Discount allowed to Debtors	13,365
Dec. 31	11,000	Goods invoiced to Branch	1,32,000
Sales – Cash	46,000	Remittances to Head Office	1,31,635
Credit	1,00,000		

It was further reported that a part of the stock (uninsured) was lost by fire during the year. Also provide for discount on closing debtors based on the years trend of prompt payment.

[Delhi, B. Com. (Hons.) I yr, 1996]

13. On February 2006, goods costing Rs. 33,000 were invoice by Calcutta head office to its branch at Kanpur and charged up at a selling price designed to produce a gross profit of 25 per cent on the selling price. At the end of the month, the return from Kanpur Branch showed that sales were Rs. 30,000. Goods invoiced at Rs. 600 to Kanpur branch had been returned to Calcutta head office. The closing stock at Kanpur branch was Rs. 12,300 at selling price.

Record the above transactions in Kanpur Branch stock a/c, Kanpur Branch adjustment A/c and Goods sent to Kanpur Branch a/c in the head office ledger and the balance the said accounts at February 28, 2006.

[Delhi, B.Com. (Pass), 1994 (B)]

14. Suresh Ltd. has one branch at Kanpur and the other at Agra, Prepare Kanpur Branch account in the books of Suresh Ltd. from the following particulars, which are related to Kanpur Branch:

Particulars	Rs.	Particulars	Rs.
Goods supplied to branch	80,000	Returns by customers	1,000
Stock opening	20,000	Wastage of stock	2,000
Debtors opening	10,000	Cash received from Debtors	58,000
Cash sales at branch	40,000	Goods returned by branch to Head Office	2,000
Credit sales at branch	60,000	Expenses of Branch	6,000
Transfer of Goods from Agra branch by Kanpur branch	4,000		
Discount allowed to customers	200		

Goods are supplied to branches by Head office at cost + 25%. All expenses of the branch are met by the Head Office and branch sends all cash received to head office.

15. M/s Goyal Brothers are having their head office at Delhi and branch at Calcutta. The following are the transactions of the Head Office with branch for the year ended 31st August, 2007:

		Rs.
Stock at branch as on 1.9.06		30,800
Debtors at the branch as on 1.9.06		16,500
Petty cash as on 1.9.06		500
Good supplied to the branch		1,51,200
Remittances from Branch:		
Cash Sales	10,500	
Realization of Debtors	1,57,740	1,68,240
Amount sent to branch:		
Salary	7,440	
Rent	2,400	
Pretty Cash	3,000	12,840
Stock at branch as on 31.8.07		23,150
Sundry Debtors at the branch as on 31.8.97		50,460
Pretty Cash as on 31.8.07		750

Show the Branch Account in the books of the head office.

16. Vasan of Chennai has a branch at Calcutta. Goods are invoiced from the Head Office at cost plus $33\frac{1}{3}\%$. Branch is allowed to make sales at invoice price only. Expenses of the branch except petty expenses are directly paid by the head office. From the following particulars, you are required to prepare the branch account to ascertain the net profit at the Branch:

Debtors as on 1.1.06	10,000	Sales : Cash	50000	
Petty Cash on 1.1.06	1,000	Credit	36000	86,000
Stock on 1.1.06 (at invoice price)	8,000	Sales returns by Debtors		800
Goods Invoiced by Head office	88,000	Goods damaged at invoice price		1,000
Furniture on 1.1.06	2,000	(amount recovered from the Ins. Co. Rs. 500)		
Cash sent by head office for pretty expenses at the branch	2,000	Depreciation on Furniture		80
Cash received by Branch to head office	70,500			
Goods returned by branch to head office	2,000	Advertisement for the branch		200
Branch Expenses:		Petty Expenses		1,500
Freight & Cartage	500			
Rent	1,000			
Salary	3,900			
Bad Debts	50			

[Delhi , B.Com (Pass), 1991]

17. A head office in Mumbai has a branch in Ahmedadad to which goods are invoiced by the head office at cost price plus 25%. All cash received by the branch is remitted to head office. All expenses are paid from Mumbai. From the following particulars, show how the branch account will appear in the books of the head office:

Stock on 1st July, 2005 (at invoice price)		12,500
Debtors on 1st July, 2005		12,000
Goods invoiced from mumbai		40,000
Remittances to Mumbai:		
Cash Sales	16,000	
Cash received from Debtors	29,500	45,500
Goods returned to the head office		2,400
Cheques received from Mumbai		

Wages and Salaries	11,000	
Rent, Rates etc.	3,000	
Sundry Expenses	500	14,500
Stock on December, 2005 (invoice price)		15,000
Debtors on 31st December, 2005		22,500

[Delhi, B.Com. (Pass), 1994]

18. Journalise the following transactions in the branch office and head office books.
    (i) Head Office has charged Rs. 5,000 as depreciation on branch assets.
    (ii) Branch has received Rs. 15,000 from a customer of Head Office.
    (iii) Goods worth Rs. 25,000 have been supplied by the branch to another branch under the advice of H.O.
19. Journalise the following transactions in the books of head office as well as branch office:
    (i) Goods worth Rs. 5000 are supplied by Delhi Branch to Agra Branch under instructions of head office.
    (ii) Delhi Branch draws a bill receivable for Rs. 5,000 on Agra branch which sends its acceptance.
    (iii) Head Office charges Rs. 4000 from Delhi branch as head office administrative expenses.
20. Show what entries would be passed by the Head Office to record the following transactions in their books:
    (a) Goods amounting to Rs. 500 transferred from Calcutta branch to Allahabad Branch under instructions from head office.
    (b) Depreciation on branch fixed assets amounting to Rs. 1,000. When such accounts are opened in the head office books.
    (c) A remittance of Rs. 3000 made by the Calcutta branch to head office on 28th December, 2006 and received by the head office on 4th January, 2007.
    (d) Goods of Rs. 5,000 sent by the head office to the Allahabad branch on 26th December, 2006 and received by the branch on 16th January, 2007.
    (e) The Calcutta branch collected Rs. 2000 from a Calcutta customer of the head office.
    (f) The Allahabad Branch paid Rs. 12000 for machinery purchased by head office in Allahabad.
21. A Delhi merchant has a branch at Chennai to which he supplies goods at cost plus 25%. The branch keeps its own sales ledger and transmits all cash received to the head office everyday. All expenses are paid from the Head Office.

    For the year ended 31st December 2006 the transactions of the branch were as follows:

	Rs.			Rs.
Stock on 1.1.06	11,000	Return Inwards		500
Debtors on 1.1.06	1,700	Cheques sent to Branch:		
Petty Cash 1.1.06	100	Rent	600	
Cash Sales	2,650	Wages	200	
Goods sent to Branch	20,000	Other Expenses	900	1,700
Collection of Ledger Accounts	21,000	Stock on 31.12.06		13,000
Goods returned to Head Office	400	Debtors on 31.12.06		2,000
Bad Debts	300	Petty Cash on 31.12.06		
Allowances to Customers	250	Including miscellaneous income of Rs. 25 not remitted to Head Office		125

Prepare Branch Trading and Profit & Loss Account and Branch Account for the year ended 31st Dec. 2006.

22. Shri Prakash of Mumbai has a ranch at Delhi. Goods are invoiced to the branch at cost plus 20%. The expenses of the branch are paid from Mumbai and the branch keeps a sales journal and the debtor ledger only.

From the information's supplied, prepare Trading and Profit and Loss a/c of the branch for the year ending 31st March 2007 and show the account of the branch as it would appear in the books of Head Office:

	Rs.		Rs.
Opening Stock (at invoice price)	12,000	Sundry Debtors on 31.03.07	4,580
Closing Stock (at invoice price)	9,000	Goods Received from Head Office	15,000
Credit Sales	20,500	Goods in Transit	
Cash Sales	8,750	(From Head office on 31.3.07)	1,800
Receipts from Debtors	18,950	Expenses paid by the head office for the branch	5,200

23. The following is the trial balance of Meerut Branch as on 31st December 2005:

Particulars	Dr. (Rs.)	Cr. (Rs.)
Delhi Head Office	3,240	
Stock, 1st January, 2005	6,000	
Purchases	97,800	
Goods Received from Head Office	19,000	
Sales		1,38,000
Goods Supplied to Head Office		6,000
Salaries	4,500	
Debtors	3,700	
Creditors		1,850
Rent	1,960	
Sundry Office Expenses	1,470	
Cash at Bank	1,780	
Furniture	6,000	
Depreciation on Furniture	400	
	1,45,850	1,45,850

Stock at branch on 31st December 2005 was valued at Rs. 7,700

Meerut Branch Account in the head office books on 31st December, 2005 stood at Rs. 460 (Debit Balance).

On 28th December, 2005 the head office forwarded goods of the value of Rs. 3700 to the branch where they were received on 3rd January, 2006.

(i) Prepare Trading and Profit & Loss Account of Meerut Branch for the year ended 31st December, 2005 and its Balance Sheet as on that date.

(ii) Pass Journal entries in the books of the head office to incorporate the above mentioned trial balance and

(iii) Show Meerut Branch Account as it would be closed in head office's ledger.

24. The following trial balance is forwarded to the London Head Office by their Branch in India. Make necessary conversion and draw up Profit & Loss a/c and the balance sheet in the books of the Head Office as on 31st December 2007:

Particulars	Dr. (Rs.)	Cr. (Rs.)
Head Office a/c		2,12,000
Remittances	48,300	
Land & Buildings	1,00,000	
Purchases	4,40,200	
Salaries	7,000	
Wages	20,000	
Plant	80,000	
Sales		6,20,000
Office Expenses	8,000	
Loose Tools	1,00,000	
Cash & Bank Balance	6,000	
Advances to Indians	14,000	
Debtors	21,000	
Bills Payable		18,500
Creditors		12,000
Stock 1.1.07	18,000	
	8,62,500	8,62,500

Stock on 31st December, 2007 was Rs. 19000. Rate of Exchange 1st January 15£. on 31st December, $16\frac{1}{2}$ £ Average rate for the year 16 £.

In the head office books the balance of Branch Account on 1st January, 2007 stood at £14600 and the balance of the remittance account at £4075.

25. A Head Office sends goods to its branch at cost plus 80% goods are sold to customers at cost plus 100% . From the following particulars ascertain the profit made at the Head Office.

	H.O. (Rs.)	Branch (Rs.)
Stock	20,000	-
Purchases	2,00,000	-
Goods sent to branch at invoice price	90,000	
Sales	2,70,000	90,000

26. A company has a branch at Hardwar, goods are invoiced to the branch at 25% profit on cost. Find out profit at branch by Debtors system.

	Rs.
Opening Balance	
Stock at Invoice Price	15,000
Debtors	9,000
Petty Cash for expenses	400
Furniture	1,200
Goods sent by H.O. at Invoice Price	80,000
Goods returned to H.O.	1,000
Goods returned by Debtors	480
Cash received from debtors	30,000
Cash Sales	50,000
Credit Sales	30,000
Discount Allowed	200
Bad Debts	100
Expenses paid by Head Office	3,900
Petty expenses paid by branch	
On Imprest system.	280
Provide depreciation on furniture	10%
Stock on 31st December at Invoice price	14,000

[Delhi, B.Com (Pass) 1990 (b)]

27. X Ltd. invoices goods to its branch at cost. From the following particulars, prepare branch account for the year ended 31st March 2006 in the books of the company.

		Rs.
Branch Stock on 1.4. 2005		33,000
Branch Stock on 31.3.2006		39,000
Branch debtors on 1.4.2005		21,000
Branch debtors on 31.3.2006		29,800
Cost of goods sent to branch during the year		1,80,000
Sales at Branch: Cash	90,000	
Credit	1,46,800	2,36,800
Cash received from Branch debtors during the year		1,38,000
Branch expenses paid by head office		10,210

28. Knight Ltd. invoices goods to its branch at selling price which is cost plus 60%. From the following figures, prepare branch account in the books of the head office:

	Rs.
Stock at branch on 1.4.2005 at invoice price	16,000
Branch debtors on 1.4.2005	14,250
Invoice price of goods sent to branch	2,08,000
Cash sales at branch	1,44,000
Credit sales	41,600
Cash expenses for the branch directly met by the head office	10,840
Discount allowed to branch debtors	650
Stock at Branch on 31.3.2006 at invoice price	22,400
Branch debtors on 31.3. 2006	7,200

ANSWERS

B. Objective type Questions

1. I (iii) II (i) III (ii) IV (ii) V (iii)
2. I (False) II (True) III (True) IV (True) V (False)

C. Exercises

			Rs.
1.	(i)	Profit	29,500
	(ii)	Cash received from debtors	55,000
2.	(i)	Deficiency of Stock	200
	(ii)	Net Profit	13,650
	(iii)	Managers Commission being 50% deficiency of stock less drawing 1000	1365-100 265 due
3.	(i)	Profit at Branch	11,700
	(ii)	Cash received from debtors	42,500
	(iii)	Opening debtors	1,000
4.	(i)	Profit at Branch	13,800
5.	(i)	Profit at Kanpur branch	82,200
	(ii)	Profit at Lucknow branch	92,800
6.		Profit at branch	32,600

7.	Profit at Branch		13,100
8.	Net Profit		21,600
9.	(i)	Net Profit	34,600
	(ii)	Closing debtors	10,000
10.	(i)	Net Profit at branch	9,700
	(ii)	Closing debtors	8,250
	(iii)	Stock reserve	3,750 3,350
11.	(i)	Credit Sales	72,000
	(ii)	Supplies from Head Office	1,50,000
	(iii)	Profit	9,200
12.	(i)	Net Profit	17,650
	(ii)	Provision for discount allowed.	1,485
13.	(i)	Net Profit	6,675
	(ii)	Shortage (Loaded price)	1,100
14.	Profit at branch		15,200
15.	Profit at Kolkatta branch		30,760
16.	Profit at branch		14,270
17.	Profit at branch		13,420
18.	Net Profit		8,195
19.	(i)	Gross Profit	15,720
	(ii)	Net Profit	10,550
	(iii)	Total of Delhi branch a/c	44,550
20.	(1)	Gross Profit	28,900
	(2)	Net Profit	20,570
	(3)	Balance Sheet	19,180
	(4)	Branch a/c	1,54,010
21.	(1)	Total of Trial Balance	£2,500
	(2)	Difference is exchange rate liabilities	
22.	(1)	Stock at the H.O. at Cost	35,000
	(2)	Stock at branch at an I.P. Price	9,000
	(3)	Profit at branch	9,000
	(4)	Profit of H.O.	1,75,000
	(5)	Provision for reserve for stock at branch	4,000
26.	(a)	Profit at branch	10,620
	(b)	Closing debtors	8,220
27.	Profit at branch		52,590
28.	(a)	Profit at Branch	1,880
	(b)	Cash received from debtors	6,600
	(b)	Cash Balance with branch	1,080

CHAPTER 18

DEPARTMENTAL ACCOUNTS

A. Essay Type Questions

1. What do you understand by departmental accounts? What are their objectives? Explain.
2. What are the advantages of departmental accounts? How the expenses are apportioned while preparing final accounts?
3. "While preparing departmental tradings Profit and Loss account apportionment of indirect expenses is necessary." Discuss such expenses and the basis on which their apportionment is made.

EXERCISES

B. Objective Type Questions

1. State whether each of the following statement is true or false.
   (a) Rent is allocated on the basis of floor area occupied by each department.
   (b) Electricity is allocated uniformly among all the departments.
   (c) General Manager salary is apportioned in all departments as per time allocated/ distributed by him.
   (d) Director's Fee is not allocated among/ between different departments.
2. Fill in the blanks
   (a) Electric Expenses are apportioned on the basis of ________ installed in each department.
   (b) Rent is allocated on the basis of________ of each department.
   (c) Bad debt is charged on the basis of ________ of each department.
   (d) Management expenses are not ________ but to be charged from General Profit and Loss a/c
   (e) Depreciation on Machinery is allocated according to the Number of ________ used / installed in each department.

C. Exercises

1. The Directors of Departmental stores Ltd. wish to ascertain, approximately, the net profit of the A, B and C departments separately for the four months ended 30th April, 2006. It is found impracticable actually to take stock on that date but an adequate system of departmental accounting is in use and the normal rates of gross profit, for the departmental concerned, are 40%, 30% and 20% on turnover, respectively. Indirect expenses are charged in proportion to departmental turnover.

   The following are the figures for each department:

	A Rs.	B Rs.	C Rs.
Stock 1.1.06	6,000	7,000	3,000
Purchases for the period	7,000	6,500	4,700
Sales for the period	12,000	10,000	6,000
Direct expenses	2,020	1,450	710

   The total indirect expenses for the period (including those relating to other departments) were Rs. 4200 on total sales of Rs. 84000.

Prepare a statement for the Directors, making a stock reserve of department on the estimated value on April 30th 2006.

2. Dinesh & sons are the owners of a departmental store. They want to ascertain the net result of three departments. A, B and c separately for the six months period ending on 30th June 2006. On this date, it was not practicable to take stock but an adequate system of departmental accounting in use and the normal rates of gross profit, for the department concerned are 30%, 25% and 20% on turnover. There are in all five departments.

The following figures are extracted from the books for the six months period ending 30th June 2006.

	A Rs.	B Rs.	C Rs.
Stock 1.1.1997	10,000	8,000	5,000
Purchases	20,000	15,000	12,000
Sales	25,000	20,000	15,000
Direct Expenses	5,000	3,000	20,00

Indirect expenses of all five departments were Rs. 10,000. The sales of all five department are Rs. 1,00,000. Indirect expenses are to be charged in proportion to departmental sales.

You are required to prepare a columnar Trading and Profit & Loss Account for the period ending 30th June, 2006 making a stock reserve for each department at 5% on estimated value of stock at 30th June 2006.

3. Shri Gangaram sells two products manufactured in his own factory. The goods are made in two department A and B for which separate sets of accounts are maintained. Some the manufactured goods of department A are used as raw materials by department B and vice-versa.

From the following particulars, you are required to ascertain the total cost of goods manufactured in departments A and B.

	Deptt. A	Deptt. B
Total units manufactured	1,00,0000	5,00,000
Total Cost of manufacturer excluding Inter departmental transfers)	10,000	5,000

Department A transferred 2,50,000 unit to Department B and the latter transferred 1,00,000 units to former.

4. From the following particulars, prepare a departmental trading and profit & loss a/c and a balance sheet as on 31st December 1995 :

	Rs.		Rs.
Capital Account	30,000	Bills Payable	1,500
Sales Dept. A	70,000	Stock 1st Jan.	
B	30,000	Dept. A	3,400
Sundry Creditors	12,000	Dept. B	1,100
General Reserve	750	Traveling Expenses	5,400
Sundry Debtors	23,000	Office Salaries	2,800
Bills Receivable	5,000	Commission	2,200
Furniture & Fittings	1,080	Advertizement	5,800
Rent, Rates and Insurance	1,800	Bank Charges	120
Marine Insurance	2,400	Printing & Stationery	2,700
Dept. A	43,000	Exchange & Discount	600
Dept. B	25,000	Postage & Telegrams	900
Cash at Bank	7050	Sundries	1,500
		Investment	6,900
		Cash in hand	2,500

Appropriate the expenses in proportion to the turnover of each department.

Closing Stock Dept. A Rs. 4000 Dept. B Rs. 1680.

5. X Ltd. has two departments A and B from the following information (particulars) prepare Departmental Trading Account and Consolidated Trading Account for the year ending 31st December 2006.

	Dept. A Rs.	Dept. B Rs.
Opening Stock at Cost	40,000	24,000
Purchases	1,84,000	1,36,000
Carriage Inward	4,000	4,000
Wages	24,000	16,000
Sales	2,80,000	2,24,000
Purchased Goods transferred :		
By Dept. B to Dept. A	20,000	
By Dept. A to Dept. B		16,000
Finished Goods transferred :		
By Dept. B to Dept. A	70,000	
By Dept. A to Dept. B		80,000
Return of Finished Goods :		
By Dept. B to Dept. A	20,000	
By Dept. A to Dept. B		14,000
Closing Stock :		
Purchased goods	9,000	12,000
Finished goods	48,000	28,000

Purchased goods have been transferred mutually at their respective departmental purchases cost and finished goods at departmental market price and that 20% of the finished stock (closing) at each department represented finished goods received from other department.

ANSWERS

B. Objective type Questions

1. (a) T (b) F (c) F (d) T
2. (a) Meters (b) Floor Area (c) Sales (d) Allocated (e) Machines

C. Exercises

	Rs.
Net Profit for departments A	1,600
And B	400
Net Loss for department C	100

[Hints. Indirect expenses are Rs. 4200 on a total sales of Rs. 84000, so of Rs. 28000, Sales expenses would be Rs. 1400 i.e., $\frac{4,200}{84,000} \times 28,000$ to be apportioned in the ratio of 12: 10: 6 or 6: 5: 3

2.	(a) Gross Profit for department		*Rs.*
		A	7,500
		B	5,000
		C	3,000
(b)	Indirect Expenses to be apportioned @ 10% on sales		
(c)	Net Loss for department	A	625
		B	400
		C	750

3. Hint - assume A and B costs of each department and then make an equation of A = 10,000 + 1/5 b and B= 5000 + ¼ a, thus costs of A and B are Rs. 8,684 and Rs. 6,316.

Rs.

				Rs.
4.	(i)	Gross Profit of	A	27,600
			B	5,580
	(ii)	Net Profit of	A	8,683
		Net Profit of	B	2,545
	(iii)	Balance of Profit & Loss appropriation a/c		3,848
	(iv)	Total of Balance sheet		50,348
5.	1.	Gross Profit Rs. 169000		A Rs. 85000
				B Rs. 84000
	2.	Reserve for unrealized profit		
		In case of	A	Rs. 2880
		In case of	B	1,440
	3.	% of Gross Profit In case of A		$\frac{85,000}{3,40,000} \times 100 = 25\%$
		% of Gross Profit In case of B		$\frac{84,000}{2,80,000} \times 100 = 30\%$

CHAPTER 19

HIRE PURCHASE SYSTEM

A. Essay Type Questions

1. What is Hire purchase agreement? Explain. [Delhi, B.Com (Pass) 2001]
2. Distinguish between Hire Purchase and Instalment System of accounting. [Delhi, B.Com (Pass) 2004]
3. What journal entries are to be made in the books of the buyer and seller, When the goods are sold on hire purchase system? And the seller takes the possession of the goods on default of payment of instalments by the hire buyer.
4. Write short note on :-
   (a) Default and Repossession in Hire Purchase. [Delhi, B.Com (Pass) 1993]
   (b) Treatment of loss on goods Repossessed. [Delhi, B.Com (Pass) 2005]

B. Objective type questions

1. Choose the correct answers from the following-
   (a) In case of hire purchase which account is debited.
      (i) Hire Vendor a/c
      (ii) Assets a/c
      (iii) None of the above.
   (b) In case of default of payment of instalment. What is the right of the vendor
      (i) Filing a suit in the court for recovery
      (ii) Repossess the goods immediately
      (iii) Filing of suit as well as repossession of goods.
   (c) Deprecation is charged by the buyer on
      (i) Cost price
      (ii) Hire purchase price
      (iii) Cost or hire purchase price whichever is less.
2. State whether the following statements ate true or false-
   (i) Incase of hire purchase the ownership of goods is passed immediately i.e. at the time of agreement.
   (ii) Interest is calculated on the purchase price
   (iii) Depreciation is charged on hire purchase price
   (iv) In case of default, the hire under is allowed to repossess the goods immediately.
   (v) Incase the price is not given, it is calculated with the help of 1st instalment.
   (vi) If the rate of interest not given, total interest is divisible equally.
   (vii) Hire purchase and instalment system are synonymous.

C. Exercises

1. Shyam purchases a Television set on hire purchase basis for Rs. 5,000 and makes the payments as the following order:

	Rs.
Down payment	1,000
1st instalment after one year of agreement	2,000
2nd instalment after two years of agreement	1,000
3rd instalment after three years of agreement	1,000

The cash price of the TV set is Rs. 4,400

Prepare necessary accounts in the books of hire vendor.

2. A purchased a truck on hire purchase system. The cash price of the truck was Rs. 74,500. He paid Rs. 20000 on signing of agreement and rest in three instalments of Rs. 20000 each. Calculate interest for each Year.

3. Bablu purchased machine on hire purchase system for Rs. 14,600, Rs. 11,400 were paid at the time of contract on 1st July, 2005 and balance was to be paid by four half-yearly instalments of Rs. 800 plus interest at 5% p.a. Depreciation charged by Bablu is 10% p.a. on diminishing balance method. Accounts are closed on 30th June. Prepare Machinery Account, Hire Vendor's Account, Interest Account and Depreciation Account in Bablu's Ledger.

4. A acquired on 1st January, 2006 a machine under a Hire Purchase Agreement which provides for five half-yearly instalments of Rs.6000 each, the first instalment being due on 1st July, 2006. Assuming that the applicable rate of interest is 10% p.a. calculate the cash value of the machine.

5. On 1st January 2006, S purchased machine from K on hire purchase basis. The particulars are as follows:

(i) Cash Price Rs.10,000, (ii) Rs. 4000 to be paid on signing the contract, (iii) Balance in three annual instalments of Rs. 2,000 cash plus interest, (iv) Interest charged on outstanding balance at 5%, (v) Depreciation at 10% p.a. on Straight Line Method. Give Journal entries and necessary ledger accounts in the books of purchaser.

6. X purchased four cars of Rs. 14,000 each on hire purchase system. The hire purchase price for all the our cars was Rs. 60,000 to be paid Rs. 15,000 down, and three instalments of Rs. 15,000 each at the end of each year. Interest is charged at 5% per annum and the buyer is depreciating cars at 10% per annum on Straight Line Method.

After having paid down payment and first instalment, the buyer could not pay second instalment and the seller took possession of three cars at an agreed value to be calculated after depreciating cars at 20% per annum on written down value method. One car was left with the buyer. The seller after spending Rs. 1,200 on repairing sold away all the three cars to A for Rs. 35,000.

Open Ledger Account in the books of both the parties.

7. X Ltd. purchased three cars from Y Ltd. costing Rs. 75,000 each on hire purchase system. Payment was to be made for each car @ Rs. 45,000 down and the balance in three equal instalments together with interest at 12% p.a. X Ltd. writes off depreciation 20% p.a. on diminishing balance. It paid the first instalment at the end of first year but could not pay they next. Y Ltd. left one car with the purchaser adjusting the value of the other two cars against the amount due. The cars were valued on the basis of 30% depreciation annually on written down value.

Show the Car a/c and Seller's a/c in the books of X Ltd. Show your calculations clearly.

8. X purchased seven trucks on hire purchase on 1.7.2006. The cash price of each truck was Rs. 50,000. He was to pay 20% of the cash purchase price at the time of delivery and the balance in five half-yearly instalments starting from 31.12.2006 with interest @ 5% per annum.

On X's failure to pay the instalment due on 30.06.2007 it was agreed that X would return three trucks to the vendor and the remaining four would be retained by him., The vendor agreed to allow him a credit for the amount paid against these three trucks less 25%.show the relevant ledger accounts in the books of X assuming that his books are closed in June every year and deprecation @ 20% is charged on Trucks.

9. Arul purchased machinery under the Hire Purchase Agreement from Babu. The cash price of the machine was Rs. 15,000. The payment for the purchase was to be made as follows: Rs. 3,000 on signing the agreement and Rs. 5,000 each at the end of first year, second year third year respectively. Calculate the amount of interest included in each instalment.

(Madras B.Com., 1997)

10. B Company purchased on 1st October, 2005 from D Company five trucks costing Rs. 5,00,000 each on hire- purchase system. Payment was to be made as follows:

10% of cash price down

25% of cash price at the end of four subsequent half - years.

Payment due on 30th September, 2006 could no be made. After negotiation, the hire - Purchaser was allowed to keep three trucks on the condition that the value of the other two trucks would be adjusted against the amount due, the trucks being valued at cost less than 25% depreciation.

B Co. closes its books on 31st March each year and depreciation charged at 15% p.a. on trucks on the original cost.

Prepare: i) Trucks Account
ii) D Company Account } In the books of Hire - Purchaser and
B Company Account in the books of Vendor.

[Delhi B.Com (Pass) 1999 (B)]

11. D. Ltd. sold three machinery costing Rs. 10,000 each to hire purchase system on 1-1-2006. P paid Rs. 6,000 on the above date to receive delivery of the machines and agreed to pay five half - yearly instalments of Rs. 6000 each.

P could not pay the third instalments instalment in time whereupon D Ltd. repossessed one machine and P retained the other two machines. The value of the returned machine was agreed to be cash price less 40%, The purchaser charges depreciation @ 10% p.a. on reducing balance method.

D Ltd. sold the repossessed machine for Rs. 4500 on 31st December 2007 after incurring repairs of Rs 200.

You are required to show:

(1) D Ltd. A/C and Machinery A/C in the books of hire - purchaser: and

(2) P's A/c and Goods Repossessed A/c in the books of D Ltd.

[Delhi B.Com (Pass) 2000]

12. From the following particulars, calculate -

(i) Value of Plant taken over by the vendor,

(ii) Value of Plant left with the Purchaser.

(iii) Profit or loss on plant taken back.

(iv) Profit or loss on plant repossessed when sold by the vendor.

Particulars

(i) X purchased 3 plants from Y costing Rs. 1,00,000 each.

(ii) X charged depreciation@ 20% on diminishing balance method.

(iii) Two plants were seized by the vendor when second instalment was not paid at the end of second year and vendor valued the plant at cost less 30% depreciation annually charged at diminishing balance method.

(iv) Vendor spent Rs. 40,000 on overhauling the plants and sold for Rs. 1,60,000.

Show the relevant ledger accounts in the books of X assuming that his books are closed in June every year and depreciation @20% is charged on plants.

Show the relevant accounts in the books of X assuming that his books are closed in June every year and depreciation @ 20% is charged on trucks.

13. Xavier purchased radio-set on hire purchase system. As per terms of agreement he is required to pay Rs. 800 down, Rs. 400 at the end of first year, Rs.300 at the end of second year and Rs. 700 at the end of third year. Interest is charged @ 5% p.a. Calculate the total cash price of the radio-set and interest paid in each instalment.

14. Oil Engines Ltd purchased a machine costing Rs. 10,00,000 on hire purchase from E.I. of India Ltd. on 1st January 2006. The amount is payable over five years with an yearly instalment of Rs. 2,00,000 Plus interest @ 10% p.a. on the straight line method. The purchasing company defaults to pay the second instalment and the vendor takes back the machine as per the agreement.

    Prepare the Machine Account and the Hire Vendor's Account.

15. X purchased a machine on 1st January 2006 on the hire purchase system. The cash price of the machine is Rs. 14,900. The terms of the agreement provided for payment of Rs.4,000 at the end of every six months over two years. The first payment was to be made on 30th June, 2006. Rate of interest was 6% per annum.

    X wrote off 10% depreciation on the reducing balance system and closed his books on the 30th June every year.

    X could not pay the instalment due on 30th June, 2007 and as a result, the hire vendor took the possession of the machine.

    Give the Machine Account in the books of X and show the loss suffered by him.

16. M/s. Raj & Bros. Purchased a motor car from Sanjaya Automobiles on 1st jan. 2006 on the Hire purchase System. The cash price of the motor car was Rs. 11,170. Rs. 3,000 was to be paid on signing the agreement and the balance in three annual instalments of Rs. 3,000 each. 5% p.a. interest is charged by the vendor. The purchaser had decided to write off 10% depreciation annually on the W.D.V. The purchaser could not pay off the instalment due on 31st Dec 2007 and as result of this, the vendor took possession of the motor car and the vendor estimated its value Rs. 5,500 and spent Rs. 400 on it. Later on, this motor car was sold for Rs. 6,400. Show the Motor Car a/c and Sanjaya Automobiles a/c in the books of M/s. Raj Bros. And M/s Raj Bros. A/c and the Repossessed Stock a/c in the books of the vendor.

17. X Limited purchased piece of machinery on 1st January, 2006 on the hire purchase system. The cash price of the machinery is Rs. 29,800. Terms of payment were Rs. 8,000 half-yearly over two years, the first payment to be made on 30th June, 2006.

    Rate of interest was 6% p.a. X Limited wrote off 10% depreciation on diminishing balance, and closed its books on 30 the June every year. It could not pay the instalment due on 30th June, 2007 and as consequence, the hire vendor took possession of the machinery.

    Give Machinery Account and Hire Vendor's Account in the books of X Limited.

18. Meenakshi Papers purchased a printing machine on 1st January, 2007 on the hire purchase system. The cash price was Rs. 15,000; payment was to be made in 4 half-yearly instalment of Rs. 4,000 each, the first payment to be made on 30th June, 2007. Interest is to be taken at 5% p.a. The Machine is to be depreciated at 15% p.a. on written down value method. Make Journal entries in the books of purchaser of machine.

19. X purchased a machine from Y for Rs. 5,60,000 payment to be made Rs. 1,50,000 down and three instalments of Rs. 1,50,000 each at the end of each year. X depreciates assets at 10% p.a. on written down value method. X depreciates assets at 10% p.a. on written down value method. Because of financial difficulties, X after having paid down payment and first instalment, at the end of the 1st year, could not pay second instalment and the seller took possession of the asset.

    Prepare the Machine a/c and Seller's a/c in the books of X and also give Purchaser a/c in the books of Y.

20. On 1st January, 2004, Engineer Ltd. purchased a machinery from Marshall on hire purchase system, over a period of three years, Rs. 5,000 were payable on delivery on 1st January 2004 and the balance by following instalments on 31st Dec. in each year.

    2004 Rs. 10,000

    2005 Rs. 10,000

    2006 Balance Amount.

Marshall charged interest at 10% p.a. on the yearly balances. The value of the machinery on delivery was Rs. 30,000. Depreciation at the rate of 20% p.a. on diminishing balances was written off in each year. Engineer Ltd. paid all the instalments on the due date.

Show the Machinery account and Marshall's Account in the books of engineer for the three years to 31st December, 2006.

21. Varun sells goods on hire purchase basis also. He fixes hire purchase price by adding 50% to the cost of the goods to him. The following are the figures relating to his hire purchase business for the year 1995:

	Rs.
Balance of Hire Purchase Stock Account as on 1st Jan. 2006	12,000
Balance of Hire Purchase Debtors Account as on 1st January, 2006	300
Selling price of goods sold on hire purchase basis during the year	90,600
Cash received from customers during the year	92,400
Total amount of instalments that fell due during the year	92,700

One customer to whom goods had been sold for Rs. 1,200 paid only three instalments of Rs. 100 each. On his failure to pay the monthly instalment of Rs. 100 due on 4th December, 2006 the goods were repossessed on 27th December, 2006 after due legal notice.

Prepare ledger accounts on Stock-Debtors System for the year ended 31st December 2006.

22. Greshams Ltd., which sells a patent product on hire purchase terms, has the following transactions for the year ended 31st December, 2006. The gross profit is 25% on Selling Price.

2006		Rs.
Jan. 1	Stock out on hire at Hire Purchase Price	4,000
	Stock on hand (in the shop)	500
	Instalments due (customers still paying)	300
Dec. 31	Stock out on hire at Hire Purchase Price	4,600
	Stock on (in the shop)	700
	Instalments due	500
	Cash received in instalments during the year	8,000

You are required to prepare necessary ledger accounts.

23. From the following detail set out the hire purchase account in the books of a trader, who sells a number of articles of comparatively small value daily on the hire purchase system. Showing his profit on this department of the business for the year ended December 31, 2006 for the purpose of charging his hire purchase customer, he adds 60% to the cost of the goods.

2006		Rs.
Jan. 1	Stock in customers hands at Selling Price	1,620
Dec. 31	Sale of the hire purchase goods during year at Selling Price	6,534
	Cash received from hire purchase customers at Selling Price	2,100
	Stock in customer's hands as Selling Price	5,674

You are required to prepare Hire Purchase Stock Adjustment Account for calculating profit.

[Delhi, B.Com. (Hons), 1997]

24. From the following data, prepare the necessary account to show the profit earned by Shiv Shankar ltd. who sells its products on hire purchase terms. Goods are sold on hire purchase at cost plus 33 1/3%.

	1st April 2005	31st March 2006
	Rs.	Rs.
Stock out at hire purchase price	3,6000	45,000
Stock in hand at shop	1,2000	10,500
Instalments due (customers still paying)	5,000	8,000

Cash received from hire purchase debtors during the year ended 31.3.2006 was Rs. 90,000.

25. A company sells goods of small value on hire purchase at cost plus 50%. From the following particulars, prepare Hire Purchase Trading Account in the books of the company.

2006		Rs.
Jan. 1	Stock out with hire purchase	9,000
	Customers at Selling Price	
	Stock at Shop (at cost)	18,000
	Instalments due	5,000
Dec. 31	Cash received from customers	60,000
	Goods repossessed (instalments not yet due Rs. 2000) as valued	500
	Instalments due, customers still paying	9,000
	Stock at shop at cost (excluding repossessed goods)	20,000
	Goods purchased during the year	60,000

[Delhi, B.Com. (Hons.) 2005 (modified)]

26. On 1st January 2006 A sold a machine to B for Rs.20,000 on hire purchase system, Rs.5,000 are paid on the date of transaction and the balance payable in three equal half-yearly instalments together with 25% p.a. on outstanding balances. A agreed to bear the cost of repair for a period of two years from the date of sale and ¼ of the profit on sale may be used for this purpose. The cost of actual repair in the First Year was Rs.200 and in the Second year it was Rs. 100.

The actual cost of the machine sold is Rs. 18,000. A closes his books on 1st December each year. Prepare necessary accounts in the books of A.

27. The Himachal Agro Farming Company acquired five tractors on hire purchase system from Punjab Tractors. Ltd. The cash price of one tractor was Rs. 10,000. The payment (price) was payable in five annual instalments of Rs.2,200 each. The first instalment was to be paid on signing the contract. The instalments concluded interest charged at the rate of 5% per annum. The farming company decided to provide depreciation @ 10% per annum to be calculated on diminishing balance method.

After paying the first and the two other instalment, the farming company discontinued payments of instalments in respect of two tractors and returned them to the Vendor. The contract, with regard to the other three tractors was, however duly carried out.

Give the necessary ledger accounts in the books of the purchasing company, Also give workings.

[Delhi, B. Com. (Hons.) 1991 (Supple.)]

28. A limited company sells a patent product on hire purchase terms. It has the following transactions for the year ending 31st March 2007.

	Rs.
1st April 2006	
Stock out on hire at hire purchase price	1,20,000
Stock on hand (at shop)	15,000
Instalment due (customers still paying)	9,000
31st March 2007	
Stock out on hire at hire purchase price`	1,38,000
Stock on hand (at shop)	21,000
Instalments due (customers still paying)	15,000
Cash received in instalments during the year	2,40,000

The business follows the practice of charging gross profit at 25 per cent of selling price.

Prepare the necessary ledger account to record these transactions in the books of the limited company in a manner as to show the cost of purchases made, the profit earned by the company during the year.

[Delhi, B.Com. (Hons.) 1st yr. 1994]

ANSWERS

B. Objective Type Questions

1. Choose the correct answers:-
   (a) II (b) II (c) I.
2. State whether True OR False.

(i) False	(v) False
(ii) False	(vi) False
(iii) False	(vii) False
(iv) True	

C. Exercises

1. Interest Rs. 343,171 and 86
2. Total Interest Rs. 5500 divisible in the ratio of 3:2:1: Rs. 2,750, Rs.1,833 and Rs. 917
3. Interest for I, II, III & IV year Rs. 80, Rs. 60, Rs. 40, and Rs. 20 Balance of Machine a/c Rs 11,826.

4.		Cash Price of Machine	Rs 25,977
5.		Balance of Machine a/c	Rs. 7,000
6.	i)	Cars a/c Rs. 11,200, Loss suffered	Rs. 6,720
7.	i)	Balance of Car a/c	Rs. 48,000
	ii)	Loss on account of default	Rs. 22,500
	iii)	Balance of sellers a/c Rs. 46,500 + 14,400 =	Rs. 60,900
8.			Rs.
	i)	Loss on account of Seizure	79,500
	ii)	Balance of Trucks a/c	1,60,000
	iii)	Balance of vendor's a/c	1,89,000
9.	I)	Total Interest	Rs. 3,000
		(divisible in the ratio of 3:2:1)	
		Rs. 1500, Rs. 1,000 and Rs. 5,00	
10.	i)	Value of 2 trucks taken over by the vendor	7,50,000
	ii)	Loss on seizure	1,00,000
	iii)	Balance of the Hire vendor a/c	10,50,000
11.	i)	Interest of Rs. 6,000 divisible in the ratio of 5:4:3:2:1 i.e. Rs. 2,000, 1,600, 1,200, 800 & 400	
	ii)	Value of 1 machine taken over by the vendor	Rs. 6,000
	iii)	Loss on seizure	Rs. 2,550
	iv)	Balance of Hire vendor a/c	Rs. 10,800
12.	i)	Value of plant taken hire by the Vendor	98,000
	ii)	Value of plant left with the purchaser	64,000

	iii)	Profit or loss on plant taken	30,000
	iv)	Profit on sale of repossessed plant	22,000
13.	i)	Cash price	2058
	ii)	Interest paid Rs. 63 + Rs. 46 + Rs. 33 =	142
14.	i)	Seizure of Machine	8,80,000
15.	i)	Interest Rs. 1,100 [Rs. 447, Rs. 340, 231, & 82]	=1,100
	ii)	Loss suffered	4,821
16.	i)	Loss on seizure	= 3,548
	ii)	Balance of the vendor's a/c	= 3,507.50
17.	i)	Interest	=2,200
	ii)	Loss suffered	= 9,642
18.	i)	Machine a/c	=10,837.50
19.	i)	Interest	=40,000
	ii)	Loss on seizure	= 1,60,267
20.	i)	Balance of Machine a/c	=15,360
21.	i)	Profit	=31,167
	ii)	Goods Repossessed	= 900
22.	i)	Profit on H.P. Trading a/c	2,050
	ii)	Goods sold on H.P.	8,800
	iii)	Purchases	6,800
	iv)	Closing stock reserve	1,150
23.	i)	Instalments due at the end	380
	ii)	Profit	930
24.	i)	Profit on H.P.	23,250
	ii)	Instalments accrued	93,000
	iii)	Goods out on hire at H.P. price during the year	1,02,000
25.	i)	Profit on H.P. purchase	20,500
26.	i)	Profit on Hire Purchase	2,000
27.	i)	Amount of interest Rs. 390, Rs. 300, Rs. 204 & Rs. 106	
	ii)	Loss on seizure of two trucks	= 3,562
	iii)	Value of two trucks seized	= 8,588
	iv)	Balance of Trucks a/c	= 24,300
28.	i)	Instalments due declaring the year	= 2,46,000
	ii)	Goods sold on H.P. at cost	= 1,98,000
	iii)	Value of purchases	= 2,04,000
	iv)	Profit	= 61,500

CHAPTER 20

PARTNERSHIP ACCOUNTS FUNDAMENTALS

A. Essay Type Questions

1. Define Partnership. State two provisions of the Indian Partnership Act, relating to partnership accounts if there is no partnership deed
2. Define partnership. What are the essential characteristics of a partnership.
3. Distinguish between:
   (i) Fixed and Fluctuating capital [Delhi, B. com (Pass) 2000(B)]
   (ii) Sacrificing ratio and gaining ratio.
4. What are the methods of calculating interest on drawings of partners?

B. Objective Type Questions

1. State whether the following statements are correct or not:-
   (I) It is necessary to have a partnership deed if partnership is formed.
   (II) It is compulsory to have a partnership deed in writing.
   (III) Minimum number of partners in a firm is two.
   (IV) Partnership comes into existence through operation of law.
   (V) Liability of partners is unlimited.
   (VI) The business of the partnership can be conducted by one partner only
   (VII) The business of the firm may be lawful.
2. In each of the following indicate which one is true -
   (I) In the absence of partnership deed:
      (a) Interest on capital is allowed
      (b) Interest on loan is allowed,
      (c) Salary to partnership is allowed
      (d) Profits and losses are divided according to their capital ratio.
   (II) The maximum number of partners in a partnership other than banking business is:
      (a) 10 (b) 50 (c) 7 (d) 20
   (III) In the absence of partnership deed, interest on loan is allowed at the rate of (a) 5% (b) 10% (c) 6% (d) 20%
3. Fill in the blanks from the following when there is no agreement -
   (I) Interest ...paid on Capital(is, is not)
   (II) Interest on loan is allowed @........(5%10% 6%)
   (III) Salary to a partner........allowed if he works more than others. (is, is not.)
   (IV) Profits and losses are shared.......(equally, unequally)
4. A and B are partners sharing profits losses in the ratio 2:1 C is admitted for 1/3 share in the business which the old partners give in their profit sharing ratio. Determine which is the new profit sharing ratio.
   (a) 3:2:1
   (b) 4:2:3
   (c) 1:1:1

C. Exercises

1. M and N are partners in a firm. M has given a loan of Rs. 8,000 to the firm on 1st April 2006. The Partnership dead is silent upon the question of provision of interest on partner's loan. Compute the amount of interest payable on the loan advanced by M to the firm assuming the books are closed on 31st December each year.
2. Amit and Vijay started a partnership business on 1st Jan. 2006. Their capital contributions were Rs. 200000 and Rs. 1,50,000 respectively. The partnership deed provided inter- alia that:

   (i) Interest on Capital @ 10% p.a.

   (ii) Amit to get a salary of Rs. 2,000 P. m. and Vijay Rs. 3,000 p.m.

   (iii) Profits are to be shared in the ratio of 3:2.

   The profits for the year ended 31st December, 2006 before making above appropriations were Rs. 2,16,000. Interest on drawings amounted to Rs. 2,200 for Amit and Rs. 2,500 for Vijay.

   Prepare Profit and Loss Appropriation Account.
3. Amar, Akbar and Anthony are partners in a firm, Amar brings Rs. 25,000 at first but withdraws Rs. 12,500 at the end of eight months. Akbar puts Rs. 15,000 at first increase it by Rs.5,000 at the end of eight months. Anthony introduces Rs. 10,000 at first and increase it by Rs. 5,000 at the end of eleven months but withdraws Rs. 5,000 at the end of five months. During the year ended 31st December 2006 they make a net profit Rs. 60,000. Show how the partners should divide this amount on the basis of the effective capital employed by each partner.

   [Adjustment after closing of Partnership Accounts]
4. A, B and C were partners in a firm sharing profit and losses in the ratio of 4:3:3. Their capitals were fixed at Rs. 1,00,000, Rs, 2,00,000 and Rs. 3,00,000. For the year 2005, interest on capital was credited to them @ 10% instead of 9% p.a. Showing your working notes clearly, pass the necessary adjustment entry.
5. P, Q and R were partner in a firm sharing profits in the ratio of 4:3:3 After division of the profits for the year ended 31.3.2006. Their capitals were Rs. 4,00,000, Rs, 3,00,000 and Rs. 2,50,000 respectively. During the year, they withdrew Rs. 15,000 each. The profit for the year was Rs. 40, 000. The partnership deed provided that interest on capital will be allowed @ 8% p.a. While preparing the final account interest on capital was not allowed.

   You are required to calculate the capitals of P, Q, and R as on 1.4.2005 and pass the necessary adjustment entry for providing interest on capitals. Show your working clearly.
6. Anita and Tina are partners sharing profits as 9:5. They agree to admit Chetan their Manager in to partnership, who is to get 1/8 share in the profits he acquires this share as 1/12 from Anita and 1/24 from Tina. Calculate new profit Sharing ratio.
7. A. B. and C were partners in firm sharing profit in the ratio of 5:4:3. B retired and his share was divided between A and C calculate new profit sharing ratio of A and C.
8. R and S are partners in a firm, sharing profits and Losses in the ratio of 3:2. They admit T as a new partner R surrenders 1/5th share of his profit in favour of T and S surrenders 5/2th of his share in favour of T. Calculate their new profit sharing ratio.

ANSWER

B. Objective Type Questions

(i) (iii) , (v) and (vii) are correct.

(ii) 1(b) II. (d) III. (c)

(iii) (c)

(iv) (i) is not (ii) 6% (iii) is not (iv) equally

(v) (b) 4:2:3.

C. Exercises

1.	Interest on Load @ 6% p.a. is allowed . Interest on loan=			Rs. 360
2.	Divisible profits Rs. 1,25,700 divisible between Amit			75,420
	And Vijay			50, 280
3.	(i) Effective Capital of Partners of Amar			2,50,000
	Akbor			2,00,000
	Anthony			1,50,000
	(ii) capital Ratio 25:20:15: OR 5:4:3			
4.	A's current a/c	Dr.	200	
	C's current a/c	Dr.	1,200	
	To A's current a/c			1,400
	(ii) Capital in the beginning Rs. 3,99,000, 3,03,000, 2,53,000			
5.	(iv) Interest on capital			Rs. 31,920, Rs. 24,240 & 20, 240.
6.	New profit sharing Ratio= 94:53:21			
7.	New profit sharing Ratio= 7:5			
8.	New profit sharing ratio= 12:6:7			

CHAPTER 21

ADMISSION OF A PARTNER

A. Essay type questions

(1) Explain the accounting treatment of '"Goodwill" When at the time of admission the new partner brings in his share of goodwill in cash. Also state the ratio in which the old partner's will share this amount of premium.

(2) Distinguish Between:

a. Revaluation Account and Memorandum Revaluation Account.

b. ' Sacrificing Ratio' and 'Gaining Ratio'.

c. Revaluation Account and Realization Account.

[Delhi, B.Com (Pass) 1999 (B), 2002 (B) & 2005]

(3) What is goodwill? Explain Super Profit and capitalisation of average profits methods of valuation of goodwill. [Delhi, B.com (pass) 1995 (B)]

(4) Explain with examples the different methods of treating goodwill in partnership books at the of time admission of a partner. [Delhi, B.com (pass) 1993]

B. Objective type questions

1. When a new partner is admitted in a firm for sharing profits/losses, point out when the admission of a partner is possible.

   (a) When it is desired by one of the partners?

   (b) When it is desired by all the partners?

   (c) When it is a directive from the govt.

   (d) None of the above.

2. When a new partner is admitted, he brings capital but does not bring cash for goodwill. What option is available to the existing partners?

   (a) Goodwill account can be opened.

   (b) Goodwill account is not opened.

   (c) None of the above.

3. When a new partner gives cash for goodwill, the amount is credited to :

   (i) Goodwill account.

   (ii) Capital account of the new partner,

   (iii) Cash account

4. if the goodwill account is raised for Rs. 20,000, then it must be debited to:

   (a) Cash account

   (b) Goodwill account

   (c) Partner's capital account

   (d) None of the above.

5. If the adjustment in the values of assets at the time of the admission of a partner shows a loss, it should be debited to the capital accounts of.

   i. The old partners in their profit sharing ratio,

   ii. All partners in their new profits sharing ratio,

   iii. The old partners in their old profit sharing ratio.

C. EXERCISES

Calculation & Treatment of Goodwill

(1) Find out the value of goodwill of the business if it is based on three years purchase of average super profits of the past 5 years, net profits during the last 5 Years were as follows:

I-Rs. 7,000, II- Rs. 6,500, III- Rs.8,000 , IV -Rs.7,500 and V- Rs. 6,000. The Capital Investment of the firm is Rs.40,000. A fair return on Capital in the market is 12 %.

(2) B and C are partners sharing profits in the ratio of 3:2. Goodwill appears in the books at Rs. 3,000. D is admitted in to partnership on payment of Rs. 20,000 for goodwill for 1/4 th share. B and C sharing profits between themselves in the same proportion as before.

a. Calculate the Sacrificing Ratio.

b. Record the transaction assuming Goodwill Account will not appear in the books of B,C and D.

(3) Brick , Sand and Cement were partners in a firm, sharing profits and losses in the ratio of 3: 2:1. following is their balance sheet as on 31st December 2006.

Liabilities		*Rs.*	*Assets*	*Rs.*
Capitals			Land and Building	50,000
Brick	30,000		Furniture	15,000
Sand	20,000		Stock	20,000
Cement	10,000	60,000	Bills receivable	5,000
Reserves		29,000	Debtors	7,500
Creditors		7,000	Cash in hand and at Bank	2,500
Bills payable		4,000		
		1,00,000		1,00,000

Lime is to be admitted as a partner with effect from 1st January 2007, on the following terms:

(a) Lime will bring, Rs. 15,000 as his capital and Rs. 12,000 as premium for goodwill. Half of the goodwill be withdrawn by the partners.

(b) Lime will be entitled to 1/6 th share in the profits of the firm.

(c) The assets will be revalued as follows:

	Rs.
Land & Buildings	56,000
Furniture	12,000
Stock	16,000
Debtors	7,000

(d) The claim of a creditor for Rs. 2,300 is paid at Rs. 2,000.

(e) Half of the reserve is to be withdrawn by the partners.

Record the Journal Entries (including cash transactions) in the books of the firm and show the opening Balance Sheet of the new firm.

(4) Gold and Silver are partners in a firm. They share profits and losses in the ratio of 4:1. following is the Balance sheet as on 31.12.2006.

Liabilities		*Rs.*	*Assets*	*Rs.*
Capital			Cash	5,000
Gold	75,000		Stock	80,000
Silver	25,000	1,00,000	Debtors	60,000
Sundry Creditors		45,000	Plant	75,000
Bills Payable		15,000		
Reserve		60,000		
		2,20,000		2,20,000

Copper now wants to join the firm. He is to pay Rs. 20,000 as premium for goodwill for 1/5th share in the future profits.

The following revaluation of the assets is agreed upon-

(i) Plant to be reduced to Rs. 60,000 , stock to Rs. 65,000 and debtors to Rs. 50,000 (Rs. 10,000 proved bad).

(ii) The new partner is to introduce 50 % of the adjusted capital of the existing partners.

Journalise the above transactions and give the opening balance sheet of the new firm.

(5) V and N were partners in a firm sharing profits in the ratio of 7:3.Their balance sheet on 31.3.2006 was as follows:

Liabilities		Rs.	Assets	Rs.
Creditors		10,000	Cash	15,500
Bills Payable		15,000	Debtors	20,000
Provision for Bad debts		500	Bills Receivables	50,000
General Reserve		10,000	Stock	30,000
P's Loan		80,000	Building	1,00,000
Capital			Land	1,00,000
V	1,50,000			
N	50,000	2,00,000		
		3,15,500		3,15,500

On 1.4.2006 they admitted P as a new partner on the following terms:

(i) P will get 1/5 th share in the profits of the firm.

(ii) P's Loan will be converted to her capital

(iii) The goodwill of the firm was valued at Rs. 2,00,000 and P brought her share of goodwill premium in cash.

(iv) provision for bad debts was to be made equal to 4 % on debtors.

(v) Stock was to be depreciated by 5 %.

(vi) Land was to be depreciated by 10 %.

Prepare Revaluation Account, Capital Accounts of V, N and P and the Balance Sheet of the new firm as on 1.4.2006.

(6) Balance Sheet of A,B and C sharing profits in ratio of 3:2: 1is given below:

Liabilities	Rs.	Assets		Rs.
A's Capital	4,00,000	Bank		40,000
B'S Capital	4,00,000	Debtors	2,00,000	
C's Capital	2,00,000	Less: Provision		
Contingency Reserve	1,20,000	For Doubtful Debts	3,000	1,97,000
Trade Creditors	1,80,000			
		Stock		2,03,000
		Furniture		30,000
		Machinery		5,30,000
		Building		3,00,000
	13,00,000			13,00,000

It was decided to admit D into partnership on the following terms and conditions:

(1) New profit sharing ratio between A, B, C and D will be 3:3:2:2

(2) Goodwill of the firm is valued at Rs. 3,00,000. D bring his share of goodwill in cash which is credited to the old partners.

(3) D brings Rs 1,50,000as his share of capital.

(4) Contingency reserve is not required any more.

(5) Provision for bad and doubtful debts to be raised.

(6) Machinery is revalued at Rs. 5,00,000 and building is revalued at Rs. 3,67,000.

Prepare Revaluation a/c Capital a/cs of A, B, C and the Balance sheet of the firm after D's Admission. Also show the calculations regarding goodwill.

(7) B and C are partners in a firm sharing profits and losses in the ratio of 5:3. They admit A into the firm on 1st April, 2006 when their Balance Sheet was as follows:

Liabilities	*Rs.*	*Assets*	*Rs.*
B's Capital	32,000	Goodwill	8,000
C's Capital	34,000	Machinery	38,000
General Reserve	8,000	Furniture	5,000
Bank Loan	6,000	Debtors	23,000
Creditors	6,000	Stock	7,000
		Bank	5,000
	86,000		86,000

Terms of A's admission were as follows:

(1) A will bring Rs. 30,000 through cheque as his share of capital and will be entitled to 1/3rd share in the profits.

(2) A is not to bring goodwill in cash. B and C raise the goodwill in the books which is valued on the basis of 2 years purchase of the average profits of the last three years .

(3) Average profits of the last three years are Rs 6,000

(4) Machinery and stock are revalued at Rs 45,000 and Rs 8,000.

(5) Goodwill is not to be shown in the books of the firm.

Prepare revaluation account, partners 's capital accounts, incorporating. the above adjustments and also. the balance sheet of the firm after the above adjustments.

(8) The following was the Balance sheet of A and B who had been sharing profits in proportion of three Fourth and one fourth, on 31St December, 2006.

Liabilities		*Rs.*	*Assets*	*Rs.*
Creditors		37,500	Cash at Bank	22,500
General		4,000	Bills receivable	3,000
Capitol accounts			Debtors	16,000
A	30,000		Stock	20,000
B	16,000		Office	1000
		46,000	Land & buildings	25,000
		87,500		87,500

They agreed to take C into partnership on 1st Jan. 2007 on the following terms.

(a) That C pays Rs. 10,000 as his capital for a fifth share in future profits.

(b) That a goodwill account be raised in the books of the new firm at a value of Rs.20,000.

(c) That stock and furniture be reduced by 10% and a 5% provision for doubtful debts be created on Debtors.

(d) That the value of land and building be appreciated by 20%.

(e) That the capital account of the partner's be re-adjusted on the basis of their profit sharing arrangement and any excess or deficiency be transferred to their current accounts

Prepare revaluation account, partner's capital accounts and the opening balance sheet of the new Firm.

(9) The following is the balance sheet of A and B as on 31.12.2006 who share profits and losses equally.

Liabilities	Rs.	Assets	Rs.
Capital :		Machinery	50,000
A	15,000	Stock	15,000
B	15,000	Debtors	10,000
Creditors	15.000	Bills Receivable	5,000
Current accounts		Cash/ bank	5,000
A	20,000		
B	20,000		
	85,000		85,000

They admit C as an equal partner on 1.1.2007 goodwill valued at Rs. 30,000. Stock to be valued at Rs. 25,000 machinery at Rs. 60,000. C is to bring in Rs. 15,000 as his capital and the necessary cash towards his share of goodwill, Goodwill account will not remain in the books.

Show necessary journal entries and also the balance sheet after admission of C.

(10) Mr. Girdhar and Mr. Gopal are partners in a firm sharing profits and losses as 5:3. The position of the firm as on 31st march 2006 is as follows:

Liabilities		Rs.	Assets	Rs.
Capital a/c			Plants & machinery	40,000
	Mr Girdhar	30,000	Stock	30,000
	Mr. Gopal	20,000	Sundry Debtors	20,000
Sundry creditors		15,000	Bill Receivable	10,000
Bank loan		42,000	Cash at Bank	7,500
		1,07,500		1,07,500

Mr. Ghanshyam now joins them on condition that he will share 3/4 th of future profit, the balance being shared by the old partners in the old ratio. He introduces Rs. 40,000 by way of capital in cash and pays off the bank loan, such amount being credited to Ghanshyam's loan a/c. He also pays Rs. 4,000 by way of premium for goodwill of the business and this amount is to remain in the business. The partners agreed to depreciate plant and machinery by 10% and raise a reserve against sundry debtors at 5%.

You are asked (1) to journalize the entries in the books of the firm and show the resultant balance sheet

And (2) to ascertain the new profit sharing ratio.

ANSWERS

B. Objective Type Questions

1.	(b)	4.	(a)
2.	(a)	5.	(i)
3.	(ii)	6.	(ii)

C. Exercises:

			Rs.
1.	Rs.6,600		
2.	Sacrificing Ratio		3:2
3.	Total of Balance Sheet		1,03,000
4.	Total of Balance Sheet		2,40,000
5.	(i)	Profit on revaluation	8,200

	(ii)	Total of Balance Sheet	3,64,000
6.	(i)	Profit on revaluation	30,000
	(ii)	Total of Balance Sheet	2,18,640
7.	(i)	Profit on revaluation	8,000
	(ii)	Total of balance sheet	1,16,000
8.	(i)	Profit on revaluation	2,100
	(ii)	Total of balance sheet	1,19,600
9.	(i)	Profit on revaluation	20,000
	(ii)	Total of Balance sheet	1,30,000
10.	(i)	New Profit Sharing Ratio	2 4:5:3
	(ii)	Total of Balance Sheet	1,46,500

CHAPTER 22

RETIREMENT OR DEATH OF A PARTNER

A. Essay type questions

1. Explain the term "retirement of a partner". Enumerate the problems, which arise at the time of retirement of a partner.
2. Treatment of goodwill on the retirement of a partner. [Delhi B.Com (Pass) 2002]
3. Enumerate the methods of treating Joint Life Policy in Partnership accounts. Explain clearly the methods in which the Joint Life Policy is shown in the Balance Sheet at its surrender value.
4. Explain the procedure of determining the amount payable to a retiring partner when he leaves the firm.
5. Give any three points of distinction between sacrificing ratio and gaining ratio.

B. Objective type questions

1. Indicate which alternative is true

1 Incase of retirement of a partner, goodwill is its full value is credited to -

(i) All partners

(ii) Only retiring partner

(iii) Only continuing partners Capital a/c

(iv) None of the above

2. Gaining ratio is calculated at the time of-

(i) Admission of a partner

(ii) Retirement of a partner

(iii) Admission as well as retirement of a partner.

(iv) None of the above

3. Profit on revaluation of assets and liabilities at the retirement of a partner is credited to -

(i) Retiring partner's capital a/c

(ii) Remaining partner's capital a/cs

(iii) All the partner's capital a/cs

(iv) None of the above

4. Insurance Premium, if it is treated as an investment, it is debited to -

(i) All partners

(ii) Profit and loss with surrender value

(iii) Profit and loss with deference between Premium paid and Surrender value

(iv) Profit and loss with Premium paid.

5. Profit or loss on revaluation of assets and liabilities is distributed among partners in the ratio-

(i) Equally

(ii) Profit sharing ratio

(iii) Capital ratio

(iv) None of the above

C. Exercises

1. A, B and C are three partners in a firm. C died on 28th Feb. 06. His share of profit from the closure of the last accounting year till the date of death was to be calculated on the basis of the average of three completed years of profits before death. Profits for 2003, 2004 and 2005 were Rs. 7000, Rs. 8000 and Rs. 9000 respectively.

   Calculate C's share of profit till the death and pass at necessary journal entry for the entry for the same.

2. X, Y and Z were partners sharing profits and losses in the ratio of ½: 1/3 : 1/6 respectively. The Balance Sheet of the firm on 31st December 2006 stood as follows:

Liabilities		*Rs.*	*Assets*		*Rs.*
Creditors		9,500	Cash at Bank		1,250
Bills Payable		2,500	Debtors	8,000	
Reserve Fund		6,000	Less Prov.	250	7,750
Capitals:			Stock		12,500
X	20,000		Motor Vans		4,000
Y	15,000		Machinery		17,500
Z	12,500	47,500	Buildings		22,500
		65,500			65,500

   Y retired on that date subject to the following conditions:

   (a) Goodwill of the firm is to be raised at Rs. 9,000

   (b) Machinery to be depreciated by 10% and motor vans by 15%.

   (c) Stock to be appreciated by 20% and Buildings by 10%

   (d) The Provision for doubtful debts to be increased by Rs. 975.

   (e) Liability for workmen's compensation to the extent of Rs. 825 is to be created.

   It was agreed that X and Z would share profits in future in the ratio of 3:2 respectively.

   You are required to prepare the Revaluation Account, Capital Accounts of the Partners and the Balance Sheet of the firm after the retirement of Y.

3. A, B and C are partners in a firm sharing profits & losses as A1/3, B1/2 and C1/6 respectively. The balance sheet of the firm as on 31st December 2006 was as follows:

Liabilities		*Rs.*	*Assets*		*Rs.*
Sundry Creditors		25,000	Land & Buildings		50,000
Loan Payable		15,000	plant & Machinery		40,000
Reserve Fund		16,000	Furniture		10,000
Capital Accounts:			Stock		25,000
A			Debtors	18,000	
B			Bed Debtors		
C	30,000		Reserve	500	17,500
	40,000		Cash in Hand		500
	25,000	95,000	Cash in Bank		8,000
		1,51,000			1,51,000

   C retires on 31st December 2006 subject to the following adjustments:

   (a) A goodwill account is to be raised in the books of the firm at Rs. 24,000.

   (b) Plant and Machinery to be depreciated by 10 per cent and Furniture by 5 per cent.

   (c) Stock to be appreciated by 15 per cent and Land & Buildings by 10 per cent.

   (d) Reserve for doubtful debts to be raised to Rs. 2,000

   You are required to pass journal entries to record the above transactions in the books of the firm and show the revaluation account the capital account of C and the Balance sheet of the new firm after B's retirement.

4. The Balance Sheet of A, B and C who were sharing profits in proportion to their capitals stood as follows on 31st December 2006

Liabilities		*Rs.*	*Assets*		*Rs.*
Sundry Creditors		6,900	Cash at Bank		5,500
Capital Accounts:			Sundry Debtors	5,000	
			Less: Prov. For Bad Debt.	100	4,900
A	20,000		Stock		8,000
B	15,000		Plant & Machinery		8,500
C	10,000	45,000	Land & Buildings		25,000
		51,900			51,900

B retired on the above date and it was agreed that

(a) Stock be depreciated by 6%.

(b) Provision for doubtful debts be brought up to 5%

(c) Land and Buildings be appreciated by 20%.

(d) A provision of Rs. 770 be made in respect of legal charges.

(e) The goodwill of the firm be valued at Rs. 10,800 (but no goodwill account is to be raised).

(f) The capital of the newly constituted firm be fixed at Rs. 28,000, each partner's share being in the new profit sharing ratio of 5/8 for A and 3/8 for C.

Show the important ledger accounts and give the Balance Sheet after B's retirement.

5. Nut, Bolt and Screw and partners sharing profits and losses in the ratio of 4:2:1. On 1st January 2006, Screw retires. On that date, the capital account of the partners showed credit balance of Nut Rs. 12,000, Bolt Rs. 10,000 and Screw Rs. 9,000. It was provided in the partnership deed that in case of retirement, the retiring partner should be entitled to a share of the goodwill of the firm to be calculated at two years purchase of the average profit of the last three years and that the payment of the capital and share of goodwill to the retiring partner shall be made by annual installment of Rs. 4,000 each, for the first two years and the Balance in the last year, interest being calculated at 10% on the unpaid balances.

The profit for the years 2003, 2004 and 2005 were Rs. 8,600, Rs. 7,600 and Rs. 4,800 respectively.

The first instalment was paid on 31st December 2006.

Show Screw's Loan Account until the payment of the whole amount due to him was made.

6. Nimu and Simu are in partnership as equal partners. Nimu by agreement retires and his son Ganu joins the firm on the basis that he would get one-third share of profit.

The balances of books of M/s Nimu and Simu were:

Liabilities	*Dr. Rs.*	*Cr. Rs.*
Goodwill	24,000	
Bank	16,000	
Debtors	6,000	
Stock	52,000	
Creditors		12,000
Capital Account:		
Nimu		46,000
Simu		40,000
	98,000	98,000

Goodwill is agreed at Rs. 60,000 and written up accordingly sufficient money is to be introduced so as to enable Nimu to be paid off and leave Rs. 8,000 in Bank Simu and Ganu are to provide such sum as to make their capital proportionate to their share of profit. Nimu agrees to contribute from his capital half of the amount Ganu has to provide.

Assuming the agreement was carried out, show the journal entries required and prepare the balance sheet of the firm of M/s Simu and Ganu.

7. On 31st December 2006 the Balance Sheet of A, B and C who share profits in the ratio of 1:2:2 was as follows:

Balance Sheet

Liabilities	*Rs.*	*Assets*	*Rs.*
Sundry Creditors	10,000	Goodwill	15,000
Capital		Debtors	10,000
A	10,000	Machinery	20,000
B	20,000	Buildings	30,000
C	20,000	Stock	10,000
General Reserve	5,000	Cash at Bank	5,000
Investment		Investment	10,000
Fluctuation Fund	3,000		
Bad Debt Reserve	2,000		
Bank Loan	30,000		
	1,00,000		1,00,000

C died on 31st March, 2007

Goodwill is to be calculated at the rate of 2 year's purchase on the basis of average of 5 years profit or loss. Profits for Jan/March 05 is t be calculated proportionately on the average profits of 3 years. The profits are 2001 Rs. 3,000, Rs. 7,000 for 2002 Rs. 10,000 for 2003 Rs. 14,000 for 2004 and a loss of Rs. 12,000 for 2005. During 2006 a moped costing Rs. 4,000 was purchased and debited to traveling account on which depreciation is to be provided @ 25% other values agreed on assets are stock Rs. 12,000, Building Rs. 35,000 and Machinery Rs. 25,000, investments valued at Rs. 8,000. Debtors are considered good.

Other values agreed on assets are stock Rs. 12,000 Building Rs. 35,000 and Machinery Rs. 25,000. Investment is valued at Rs. 8,000 Debtors are considered good.

Prepare New Balance Sheet of the firm, Journal Entries and Ledger Accounts of the partners.

8. The following is the Balance Sheet of the firm of A, B, C as on 31.12.2006 Their profits sharing ratio is 3:2:1:

Liabilities		*Rs.*	*Assets*	*Rs.*
Capitals a/c:			Fixed Assets	40,000
A		16,000	Sundry Debtors	32,000
B		12,000	Insurance Policy	
C		10,000	On joint life or partners	6,000
Capitals a/c:			Stock	24,000
A		4,000	Bank	9,000
B		3,000	Cash	3,000
C		1,000		
Reserve		18,000		
P & L a/c				
Opening Balance	6,000			
+ Surplus	14,000	20,000		
Creditors		20,000		
Bank Overdraft		10,000		
		1,14,000		1,14,000

B died on 31.3.07. His account has to be settled and paid for the year 2007 proportionate profit of 2006 is to be taken into account. For 2006, a bad debt of Rs. 2,000 has to be adjusted. Goodwill has to be calculated 3 times of the four years average profits. A policy is taken on the joint life of partners for Rs. 35,000 and the annual premium of Rs. 2,000 ha to be paid on February every year. The profits for 2006 Rs. 16,000, 2005 Rs. 20,000 and 2004 Rs. 12,000. Goodwill account need not be kept in accounts. Calculate the amount payable to B's heirs. Show necessary ledger accounts of all partners and other detailed calculations.

9. A, B and C were partners sharing profits and losses in the ratio of 5:3:2. It was provided in the partnership deed that in the event of death of a Partner, his legal representatives would receive:

(a) the balance at the credit of his capital account as at that date:

(b) his share of goodwill as calculated on the basis of three year's purchase of average profits of the previous four years.

(c) His share of profit for the year, calculated on the basis of profit of the previous year for e period beginning from the date of last accounting year till the date of death.

A died on 31st March 2006. His capital as on 1st January, 2006 was Rs. 25,000. Profits of the firm were 2002 Rs. 5,000, 2003 Rs. 5,500, 2004 Rs. 7,000 and 2005 Rs. 8,000. The lives of the partners were severally insured as follows :- A - Rs. 20,000, B-Rs. 10,000, C- Rs. 6,000. The premiums were charged to Profit and Los Accounts. The surrender value of the policies as on 31st March 2006 was 40% of the face value.

Prepare A's Executive a/c

ANSWERS

B. Objective type Questions

1 (i) 2 (ii) 3 (iii) 4 (ii)

C. Exercises

		Rs.
1.	Share of C	444.95
2.	(i) Profit on Revaluation	6,000
	(ii) Total of Balance Sheet	75,925
3.	(i) Profit on Revaluation	2,750
	(ii) Capital Accounts	
	A	44,250
	B	61,375
	C	32,125
	(iii) Total of Balance Sheet	1,77,750
4.	(i) Profit on Revaluation	3,600
	(ii) Total of Balance Sheet	55,470
5.	(i) Screws Capital a/c	11,000
	(ii) Interest I year	1,100
	II year	810
	III year	491
6.	(i) Cash brought of Simu	18,000
	(ii) Total of Balance Sheet	1,26,000
7.	(i) C's executors a/c	27,700
	(ii) Capital a/c of A	13,600
	(iii) Capital a/c of B	27,200
	(iv) Total of B/S	,08,500
8.	Amount payable to heirs	52,000
9.	Balance payable to A's executor	42,763

CHAPTER 23

DISSOLUTION OF A PARTNERSHIP FIRM

A. Essay Type Questions

1. What do you understand by the term 'Premium' Explain the treatment of goodwill in partnership accounts.
2. Explain Garner vs. Murray Rule

   [Delhi, B. Com. (Pass) 2001, 2004]
3. Explain the working of Gamer Vs. Murray decision. Does it apply in India? How are the partners become affected if this decision does not apply?
4. Distinguish between:
   (a) Dissolution of Partnership and dissolution of Partnership firm. [Delhi, B.Com. (Pass) 2006]
   (b) Firm's debt and Private Debt
   (c) Realisation Account and Revaluation Account [Delhi, B.Com. (Pass) 2002 (B), 2004]

B. Objective Type Questions

1. Point out which account is debited at the time of dissolution of a firm when assets are transferred:
   (i) Revaluation Account
   (ii) Realisation Account
   (iii) Profit and Loss Adjustment a/c
   (iv) None of the above.
2. When assets are realised who is paid first?
   (i) Partners Capital a/c
   (ii) Partners Loan a/c
   (iii) Creditors
   (iv) Expenses relating to dissolution
3. If a partner is insane, partnership firm is dissolved, explain which is the mode of dissolution -
   (i) Dissolution by Agreement
   (ii) Compulsory Dissolution
   (iii) Dissolution by Court
   (iv) Dissolution by Notice.
4. The Partnership firm is dissolved if number of its partners exceeds
   (i) 5 (ii) 10
   (iii) 20 (iv) 50
5. The firm is dissolved if it deals in -
   (a) Unlawful business
   (b) Lawful business
   (c) Lawful in the beginning but subsequently becomes illegal.
   (d) None of the above.

C. Exercises

1. Given below is the Balance Sheet of M/s A, B and C as on 31st December 2006.

Liabilities	Rs.	Assets	Rs.
Sundry Creditors	4,000	Cash	100
A's Loan	1,000	Stock	2,400
Capital Accounts:		Debtors	2,000
A	500	Furniture	300
B	300	C's Capital Overdrawn	1,000
	5,800		5,800

Due to the inability to pay the creditors, the Partnership firm is dissolved. B and C can not pay anything. A can contribute only Rs. 150 from his private estate. Stock realizes Rs. 1,500, Debtors realize Rs. 1,600 and Furniture is sold Rs. 100. Expenses on realisation amount to Rs. 300.

Prepare Ledger Accounts to close the books of the firm.

2. The Balance Sheet of A, B and C who are sharing profits and losses in the ratio of 2 : 2 : 1 is as follows on 31st March 2006 the date of dissolution.

Liabilities	Rs.	Assets	Rs.
Sundry Creditors	1,20,000	Cash	1,000
Bank Loan (With a charge on stock)	50,000	Stock	60,000
Capital Accounts:		Other Assets	1,09,000
A	30,000	Goodwill	30,000
B	20,000	Capital a/c	20,000
	2,20,000		2,20,000

Stock realized Rs. 52,000 and other assets were sold for Rs. 90,000, expenses on realization amounted to Rs. 3,000. Assuming that all the partners are insolvent, prepare the necessary ledger accounts to close the books of the firm.

3. On 1st January 2006 Abhitab and Ajitabh agreed to take Abhishek into partnership. It was also agreed that he would bring Rs. 5,000 as his capital and that Abhitabh and Ajitabh's capitals would be Rs. 15,000 and Rs. 10,000 respectively. Their profit sharing ratio would be 1/2 to Abhitabh and 1/2 to Ajitabh and Abhishek each respectively. On 30th November 2006, the partnership is dissolved. On this date their Balance Sheet was as follows:

Liabilities	Rs.	Assets	Rs.
Sundry Creditors a/c	10,000	Land & Building	15,000
Abhitabhs's Capital a/c	15,000	Plant & Machinery	12,000
Abhitabh's Current a/c	1,000	Stock	10,000
Ajitabh's Capital a/c	10,000	Debtors	3,000
Ajitabh's Current a/c	500	Abhishek's current a/c	500
Abhishek's Capital a/c	5,000	Cash at Bank	1,000
	41,500		41,500

On the date of dissolution:

a. Abhitabh agreed to take Land and Buildings at an agreed valuation of Rs. 20,000.

b. Value of Goodwill sold Rs. 10,000

c. Remaining assets were sold at their book values.

Prepare Realization Account, Partners Capital Accounts and Bank Account also state the amount which each partner would get from the firm.

d. A and B are partners in a firm sharing profit and losses in the ratio of 3 : 1. Their Balance Sheet as on 30th September 2006 was as follows:

Liabilities		Rs.	Assets		Rs.
Creditors		11,200	Cash		3,500
Bills Payable		1,800	Stock		17,800
A's Loan		5,000	Debtors	13,800	
Reserve Fund		6,000	Less: Provision	1,400	12,400
Capital Fund:			Furniture		2,800
A	15,000		Plant and Machinery		22,500
B	20,000	35,000			
		59,000			59,000

They decide to dissolve the firm, the assets realized as follows:

Stock Rs. 18,200, Debtors Rs. 10,600, Furniture Rs. 1,800, P1ant & Machinery Rs. 19,000.

Creditors allowed a discount of 2% and expenses of realization amount to Rs. 544. Prepare the necessary accounts to close the books of the firm.

5. Amir, Abhishek and Anurag sharing profits in the ratio of 3 : 1 : 1 agree upon dissolution that they would take over certain assets and liabilities and carry on business separately.

Liabilities	Rs.	Assets		Rs.
Creaditors a/c	6,000	Cash a//c		3,200
Loans a/c	1,500	Sundry Assets a/c		17,000
Capitals: Amar a/c	27,000	Debtors a/c	24,200	
Abhishek a/c	10,500	Less: Provision for Bad debts	1,200	23,000
Anurag a/c	7,000	Stock a/c		7,800
		Fixtures a/c		1,000
	52,000			52,000

a. Goodwill is to be ignored.

b. Amar is to take over all fixtures at Rs. 800, debtors amounting to Rs. 20,000 at Rs. 17,020. The creditors of Rs. 6,000 is to be assumed by Amar at that figure.

c. Abhishek is take over all the stock at Rs. 7,000 and certain of the Sunday assets at Rs. 7,200 (being book value less 10%).

d. Anurag is take over remaining Sunday assets at 90% of the book values less Rs. 100 allowance and assume responsibility for the discharge of the loan together with interests of Rs. 30 (accruing) which has not been recorded in the books of the firm.

The expenses of dissolution were Rs. 270.

The remaining debtors were sold to a Debt collecting agency for 50% of the book values.

Prepare necessary ledger accounts to close the books of the firm.

6. P, Q, R and S are partners sharing 4 : 3 : 2 : 1. Their position statement was as follows:

Liabilities	Rs.	Assets	Rs.
Bank Loan	20,000	Cash	1,500
Creditors	40,000	Building	44,000
P's Capital	30,000	Stock	60,000
Q's Capital	20,000	R's Capital	3,500
		S's Capital	1,000
	1,10,000		1,10,000

The firm is dissolved .All assets realized Rs. 82,000. All outside liabilities paid Rs. 58,500 in full satisfaction. Outstanding creditors are also paid Rs. 500. The expenses of dissolution are Rs. 600. S becomes insolvent and R paid only Rs. 3,000. Prepare ledger accounts to close the books of the firm.

7. Ram, Shyam and Hari were partners sharing profits and losses in ratio of 2 : 2 : 1. On January 1, 2006 their Balance Sheet was as follows:

Liabilities	Rs.	Assets		Rs.
Capital		Cash at Bank		24,400
Ram	30,000	Debtors	16,000	
Shyam	24,000	Less: Provision	400	15,600
Hari	12,000	Stock		12,000
Reserve	10,000	Furniture		4,000
Creditors	24,000	Building		44,000
	1,00,000			1,00,000

The firm was dissolved on that date. The assets realized are follows:

	Rs.		Rs.
Debtors	14,000	Stock	10,000
Furniture	2,000	Building	50,000

The creditors were settled for Rs. 22,000. It was found, however, that there was a liability for Rs. 6,000 for damages, which had to be paid. Realization expenses amounted to Rs. 2,000.

Prepare realization Account, Partners capital Account and the bank Account to close the books of the firm.

8. Gopal, Govind and Ghanshyam were partners sharing profits as to 3/6th, 2/6th and 1/6th. Their Balance sheet on 30th June 2006 stood as follows:

Balance Sheet

Liabilities	Rs.	Assets	Rs.
Bank Overdraft	50,000	Cash at Bank	2,000
Sundry Creditors	40,000	Bills Receivable	4,000
Capital Accounts:		Debtors	20,000
Gopal	28,000	Stock	40,000
Govind	7,000	Machinery	30,000
		Capital a/c Ghanshyam	29,000
	1,25,000		1,25,00

The firm was dissolved on 30th June, 2006 when all the partners become insolvent, the assets realized Rs. 71,000. The expenses on dissolution were Rs. 1,000.

Prepare the necessary Ledger Account showing the final adjustments.

9. Ram, Shyam and Mohan are partners sharing profits as to 2 : 2 : 1. Their Balance Sheet as at 30th June 2006 is as follows:

Liabilities		Rs.	Assets	Rs.
Creditors		4,000	Bank	5,000
Capitals:			Debtors	4,000
Ram	10,000		Stock	5,000
Shyam	4,000		Fixtures	2,000
Mohan	2,000	16,000	Machinery	9,000
Reserve found		5,000		
		25,000		25,000

They decided to dissolve the business. The following are amounts realized: Machinery Rs. 8,500 Fixture Rs. 1,500, Stock Rs. 7,500 and Debtors Rs. 3,700. Creditors allowed a discount of 2% and Ram agreed to bear all realization expenses. For this service Ram is plaid Rs. 120. Actual expenses amount to Rs. 900 which was withdrawn by him from the firm . There was an unrecorded asset of Rs. 500 which was taken over by Shyam at Rs. 400.

Prepare Realization. Bank and Partners' Capital Accounts.

10. The following is the Balance Sheet of Raju, Anand and Deepak as at 31st December 2006

Liabilities		Rs.	Assets	Rs.
Creditors		1,02,400	Bank	5,500
Loan:	Raju	30,000	Debtors	96,060
	Anand	12,000	Stock	64,000
Current a/c:			Machinery	28,600
	Raju	21,200	Land	84,000
	Anand	250	Current a/c Deepak	9,940
Capital:	Raju	60,000		
	Anand	40,000		
	Deepak	20,000		
		2,88,100		2,88,100

On account of heavy losses in the past two years, it is decided to close the business. The assets with the exception of Bank balance realized Rs. 2,26,880. The firm has to pay Rs. 1,500 for an outstanding bill not recorded in the books. Partner Deepak becomes insolvent and nothing is received from him.

Prepare necessary accounts to close the books of the firm.

11. Premnath, Ramnath and Loknath were partners in M/s Lok Pran & co. sharing profits and losses in the ratio of 2 : 2 : 2. They decide to convert their business into a private

company with effect from September1, 2006 on which date their Balance Sheet stood as under:

Liabilities		Rs.	Assets	Rs.
Partner' Account			Goodwill	8,000
Prem Nath	2,500		Motor Car	5,000
Lok Nath	8,500	11,000	Commission Receivable	1,000
Loan from Lok Nath		5,000	Stock	4,000
Bank Overdraft		3,000	Debtors	8,000
Creditors		6,000	Cash	1,000
Bills of Exchange		5,000	Ram Nath's a/c	3,000
		30,000		30,000

All assets (except cash and commission receivable which is irrecoverable) and all outside liabilities are taken by the company for a consideration of Rs. 20,000 to be discharged of Rs. 10 each, treated as fully paid in the limited company.

Show, Ledger Account to close the books of the firm.

12. B, K V and S were partners sharing profit and losses in the ratio of 3 : 3 : 2 : 2 respectively. The following is their Balance Sheet at 31st December 2006.

Liabilities		Rs.	Assets		Rs.
Creditors		31,000	Cash in hand		4,000
B;s Loan		20,000	Debtors	32,000	
Capital Account:			Less: Provision		
B	40,000		Bad debts	1,000	31,000
K	30,000	70,000	Stock		20,000
			Furniture		8,000
			Car		14,000
			Capital Accounts:		
			V	12,000	
			S	32,000	44,000
		1,21,000			1,21,000

It was decided to dissolve the firm effect from December 31, 2006 and K was appointed to liquidate the assets and pay the creditors. He was entitled to receive 5% commission on the amount paid to another partner towards capital. He was to bear the realization expenses which amounted to Rs. 500.

The assets realized Rs. 54,000 excluding cash in hand. Creditors were paid in full. In addition a sum of Rs. 5,000 was also paid to staff on retrenchment in full settlement of their claim.

S was insolvent and the partner accepted Rs. 7,400 from his estate in full settlement.

Applying the Rule in the leading case of Garner vs. Murray, prepare the necessary Ledger Accounts and close the books of the firm.

[Delhi B.Com. (Hons.) 1yr, 2000]

13. P, Q and R are partners sharing profit in the ratio 5 : 3 : 2. Their Balance Sheet is as follows:

Liabilities	Rs.	Assets	Rs.
Creditors	11,500	Buildings	3,000
General Reserve	5,000	Stock	13,000
P's Capital	10,000	Debtors	19,000
Q's Capital	8,000	Cash	1,000
R's Capital	1,500		
	36,000		36,000

Due to financial crisis the firm was dissolved. The assets realized for Rs. 19,950. Creditors accepted Rs. 10,450 in their full settlement, Realization expenses Rs. 1,000. R became insolvent and only Rs. 100 are received from him.

Prepare Ledger accounts following the rule of Garner vs. Murray's case.

[Delhi, B.Com. (Pass) 1990 (Supplementary)]

14. D, E and F were partners. Their profit sharing ratio was 4 : 2 : 3. They dissolved their firm. The Balance Sheet on that date was as follows:

Liabilities	Rs.	Assets	Rs.
D's Capital	34,000	Plant	30,000
E's Capital	23,000	Machine	13,850
F's Capital	1,500	Stock and Debtors	25,200
E's Loan	1,000	Cash	6,550
Bills Payable	7,550		
Profit & Loss Account	8,550		
	75,600		75,600

Assets were sold for Rs. 50,100. Realization expenses were Rs. 300. F became insolvent and only Rs. 512 were received from him.

Prepare necessary ledger accounts following the rule of Garner vs. Murray's Case.

[Delhi, B.Com (Pass) 1991 (Correspondence Course)]

15. Bhaskar, Charan and Desai are equal partners. Their Balance Sheet as on 31st March 2006 stood as follows:

Liabilities	Rs.	Assets	Rs.
Creditors	55,000	Cash at Bank	6,250
Capital Accounts		Debtors	62,500
Bhaskar	82,500	Stock	87,500
Desai	55,000	Investments	25,000
		Furniture	1,250
		Charan's Capital a/c	10,000
	1,92,500		1,92,500

The firm was dissolved as on that date. For the purpose of dissolution, the investments were valued at Rs. 57,500 and stock at Rs. 70,000. Desai agreed to take over the investments and Bhaskar to take over stock. He also took over the furniture at book value. The debtors realized Rs. 59,000 and creditors were paid off at Rs. 53,500 in full satisfaction of their claims.

Assuming that Charan is insolvent and is unable to bring in anything in respect of his debts to the firm, show the Realization Account, Capital Accounts and Bank Account, the final adjustments being made in accordance with decision in Garner vs. Murray.

16. A, B and C are in partnership sharing profits and losses three sixths, two sixths and one sixth respectively. The state of affairs on the date of dissolution was as follows:

Balance Sheet

Liabilities	Rs.	Assets	Rs.
Sundry Creditors	38,500	Cash in Hand	9,860
A's Loan Account	2,750	Sundry Debtors	30,560
Capital Accounts:		Stock	18,440
A	15,200	Furniture	7,200
B	11,200	C's Capital a/c	1,590
	67,650		67,650

The assets realized: Stock Rs. 13,840, Furniture Rs. 5,150 and Debtors Rs. 29,200. The creditors were paid less discount amounting to Rs. 250. A and B are solvent but C is insolvent and he is unable to bring in anything. The expenses of winding up were Rs. 520.

Prepare Realization Account, Cash Account and Capital Accounts of the partners.

17. The following was the Balance Sheet of M/s Ideal Works in which A, B and C were partners showing profits and losses in the ratio of 6 : 3 : 5.

Balance Sheet of M/s Ideal Works as at 31.3.2006

Liabilities	Rs.	Assets	Rs.
A's Capital a/c	25,000	Land & Building	10,000
C's Capital a/c	15,000	Furniture	5,000
A's current a/c	1,000	Stock in Trade	23,100
C's Current a/c	500	Sundry Debtors	30,000
Sundry Creditors	30,000	Cash at Bank	2,500
Loan on Mortgage of		B's Current a/c	4,900
Land & Building	4,000		
	75,500		75,500

It was decided to dissolve the partnership as on the date of the Balance Sheet. The assets of the firm realized as under:

Land & Building Rs. 6,000, Furniture Rs. 2,000, Stock in trade Rs. 15,000 and Sundry Debtors Rs. 20,000. The expenses of realization amounted to Rs. 2,000. The Sundry Creditors agreed to receive 75 paise in a rupee in full satisfaction of their claims. Loan on Mortgage was paid. It was ascertained that B has become insolvent. B's estate had contributed only 50 paise in a rupee.

Write up Realization Account, Bank Account, Capital a/c and Current Accounts of the partners following the rule given in Garner vs. Murray.

18. A, B and C were in partnership sharing profits & loses in the ratio of 2 : 3 : 5. They prepared the following balance sheet on 31.12.06 when they decided to dissolve.

Balance Sheet
(as on 31.12.2006)

Liabilities		Rs.	Assets	Rs.
Loan from bank		3,00,000	Plant & Machinery	5,00,000
(Against the security of			Debtors	50,000
Plant Machinery)			Stock	50,000
Loan from C		40,000	Advance to A	40,000
Trade creditors		2,50,000	Cash	10,000
Bills Payable		10,000	Profit and Loss a/c	1,50,000
Capital:			(Debit Balance)	
A	60,000			
B	80,000			
C	60,000	2,00,000		
		8,00,000		8,00,000

Plant and Machinery realized Rs. 3,50,000, Debtors Rs. 30,000 and Stock Rs. 40,000. A has a private estate, valued at Rs. 1,00,000 and his liabilities amounted to Rs. 40,000. The private estate realized only Rs. 60,000. B is insolvent, C can pay only 50 paise in a rupee of what is payable on his own account to the firm.

Prepare necessary ledger accounts, assuming that the loss on realization is to be determined after considering the amount ultimately paid to all the creditors.

[Delhi, B.Com. (Hons.) I Yr. 1988, modified]

19. The following was the Balance Sheet of A and B as on 31st December 2006.

Liabilities		Rs.	Assets	Rs.
Sundry Creditors		16,000	Cash at Bank	1,000
Capital Accounts:			Sundry Assets	95,000
A	40,000			
B	40,000	80,000		
		96,000		96,000

On this day they agreed to sell their business to X Y Co. Ltd. The company took overall the assets except Cash at Bank for Rs. 1,00,000. The purchase price was paid by issue of 7,000 shares of Rs. 10 each at a premium of Rs. 2 per share fully paid up and the balance in cash. Creditors were paid by the firm Rs. 15,000 in full settlement of their claims.

Prepare Realization Account and close the books of A and B and pass Journal entries to record the above in the books of X Y Co. Ltd.

20. X, Y and Z sharing profits in the proportion of 3 : 2 : 1 agreed upon the dissolution of partnership on 31st December 2006 on which date their Balance Sheet was as under:

Liabilities		Rs.	Assets		Rs.
Capital Accounts:			Machinery		40,500
X	40,000		Stock		7,550
Y	20,000	60,000	Investments		20,830
Mrs. X's Loan		10,000	Joint Life Policy		14,000
Creditors		18,500	Debtors	9300	
Life Policy Fund		14,000	Less: Provision	600	8,700
Investment Fluctuation Fund		6,000	Z's Current a/c		11,500
			Bank Balance		5,420
		1,08,500			1,08,500

The Investments are taken over by X for Rs. 17,500. X agrees to discharge his wife's Loan. Y takes over all stock at Rs. 7,000 and debtors amounting to Rs. 5,000 at Rs. 4,500. The remaining debtors realize 50% of their book values. Machinery is sold for Rs. 55,000 the expenses of realization amount to Rs. 600.

It is found that an investment not recorded in the books is worth Rs. 3,000. The same is taken over by one of the creditors at that value.

Pass Journal entries to close the books of the firm.

21. Ramesh and Mahesh were in partnership sharing profits in the ratio of 3 : 1. They agreed to dissolve the firm. The assets realized Rs. 1,60,000. The liabilities of the firm were as follows:

Creditors Rs. 90,000, Loan from Ramesh Rs. 40,000, Ramesh Capital Rs. 20,000 and Mahesh's Capital Rs. 30,000.

Show by means of accounts the distribution of cash received.

22. Anila, Kapila and Pramila were partners sharing profits and losses in the ratio of 4, 3 and 3 respectively. Their respective capitals on 1st January, 2006 were Rs. 15,000 Rs. 12,000 and Rs. 9,000. Under agreement capitals carried interest at 5 per cent per annum. During 2006 and 2007, the profit before, allowing interest on capitals, were Rs. 6,000 and Rs. 7,500. Each partner's drawings were Rs. 1,500 per year.

On 31st December, 2007, when creditors amounted to 20 per cent of the total assets, the partnership was dissolved and creditors were paid out Rs. 10,000 in full satisfaction. The assets realized Rs. 39,000.

Show necessary Ledger Accounts to close the books of the firm.

23. Describe the method of distribution of cash among partners after dissolution of a firm. Rajendra and Anil were in partnership and agreed to dissolve. The assets realized Rs. 70,000. The liabilities were as follows: Sundry Creditors Rs. 45,000. Loan from Rajendra Rs. 20,000. Rajendra's Capital Rs. 10,000 and Anil's Capital Rs. 15,000.

Show by means of accounts, how the cash realized should be distributed.

ANSWERS

B. Objective Type Questions

1. (ii) 2 (d) 3 (iii) 4 (iii) 5 (a)

C. Exercises

			Rs.
1.	(i)	Loss on Realisation	1,800
	(ii)	Creditors are paid	3,150
2.		Loss on Realisation	60,000
3.	(i)	Profit on Realisation	15,000
	(ii)	Balance of Capital a/c	
		Abhitabh	3,500
		Ajitabh	14,250
		Abhishek	8,250
4.	(i)	Loss on Realisation	6,220
5.	(i)	Loss on Realisation	5,300
	(ii)	Cash payable	12,000
6.	(i)	Loss on Realisation	21,600
	(ii)	Loss of S	3,160
		Loss of R	5,522
7.	(i)	Loss on Realisation	5,600
	(ii)	Total of Cash a/c	1,00,400
8.		Bank Overdraft and creditors are paid off rateably i.e. 80 Paise in a rupee	
9.	(i)	Profit on dissolution	1,560
10.	(i)	Loss on realisation	47,280
	(ii)	Deficiency of Deepak	5,700
11.	(i)	Profit on realisation	9,000
12.	(i)	Loss on realisation	24,000
	(ii)	Commission to K	762
13.		Loss on realisation	15,000
14.		Loss on realisation	19,250
15.	(i)	Profit on realisation	13,000
	(ii)	Loss of Charan	5,667
16.		Loss on realisation	8,280
17.		Loss on realisation	19,600
18.	(i)	Loss on realisation	76,667
	(ii)	C's Share of Loss on realisation	6,667
19.		Profit on realisation	6,000
20.		Profit on realisation	28,970
21.		Loss on realisation	20,000
22.		Loss on realisation	11,500

23. (i) Cash is distributed on the basis of maximum loss, then Anil would get Rs. 5,000 after creditors and Rajendera's loans are repaid .

(ii) If cash is distributed on the basis of capital ratio, then Anil would get Rs. 3000.